A Doctor's Life

Unique Stories

William T. Close, M.D.

MEADOWLARK SPRINGS PRODUCTIONS

Published by:
Meadowlark Springs Productions
P.O. Box 4460
Marbleton, Wyoming 83113

A Doctor's Life: Unique Stories
By William T. Close, M.D.

Expanded Revised Edition
Second Printing 2001

Previous editions published by Ballantine Books, New York.

Copyright © 2001 by William T. Close, M.D.

Foreword copyright © 1996 by Glenn Close.

Publisher's Cataloging-in-Publication
(*Provided by Quality Books, Inc.*)

Close, William T.
 A doctor's life : unique stories / William T. Close.
— Expanded rev. ed.
 p. cm.
 ISBN: 0-9703371-0-8

 1. Close, William T. 2. Physicians—United States—Biography.
 I. Title.

R154.C365A3 2001   610'.92
                                  QVI00–782

Book design by Christine Nolt, Cirrus Design, Santa Barbara, California

Cover design by Peri Poloni, Knockout Design, Cameron Park, California

Cover photo of Dr. Close by Carole Bardin, Photographer,
Western Art Gallery and Studio, Pinedale, Wyoming

Book production coordinated by Gail Kearns,
GMK Editorial & Writing Services, Santa Barbara, California

Dr. Close acknowledges that the Department of Family and Preventative Medicine, University of Utah School of Medicine published an earlier edition of this Work for medical school teachers and students in 1994 under the title *The Earth Is Not a Resting Place.* Dr. Close also acknowledges and thanks Neal Whitman, Ed.D., and Elaine Weiss, Ed.D., for their vision that made the initial work possible.

Printed in the United States of America

A Doctor's Life

This book is dedicated to my children,

Tina, Glennie, Alexander, Jessie

*While it may be comforting to imagine a life free of stresses and strains in a carefree world, this will remain an idle dream . . . Man could escape danger only by renouncing adventure, by abandoning that which has given to the human condition its unique character and genius among the rest of living things. Since the days of the cave man, the earth has never been a Garden of Eden, but a Valley of Decision where resilience is essential to survival. **The earth is not a resting place.** Man has elected to fight, not necessarily for himself, but for a process of emotional, intellectual, and ethical growth that goes on forever. To grow in the midst of dangers is the fate of the human race, because it is the law of the spirit.*

—RENÉ DUBOS,
Mirage of Health: Utopias,
Progress and Biological Change

CONTENTS

Foreword

IN MY EARLIEST CHILDHOOD, my father was a dashing, elusive figure. He worked in "the City," which meant that he had to commute back and forth from our home in the country, leaving before sunrise and returning late at night. I knew that he was a doctor. That word was magic and exciting. My father was different. He was doing special and important things. In those days he was always exhausted when he came home, and we were told that we must be very quiet because "Daddy is sleeping." I remember peering cautiously into my parents' bedroom and seeing my father asleep, bathed in the eerie light of an infrared heat lamp. He was handsome and vital, and always deeply sympathetic to the suffering of any creature, human or otherwise. Our house in those early days was overrun by a motley assortment of New York City street dogs that my dad periodically rescued from the labs at his medical school.

His was the kind of vitality that immediately changed the chemistry of whatever space he entered—a true life force. That has not changed. Today he is as restless and alive as he is in my earliest memories. He is a born physician, a person skilled in the art of healing, and he is brilliant.

I am now in my middle years, sixteen years older than my parents when they first went to Africa. As I face each day trying to achieve that precarious balance between family and career, I have nothing but the deepest love and respect for the two people who brought me and my three siblings into this world. Yes, they are flawed. Who isn't?

Yes, mistakes were made. What family doesn't have its own particular quota of pain? But my parents have never given up their extraordinary idealism, their sense of service to, and responsibility for, their fellow human beings—their respect for all life. I am moved by my father's enthusiasm, knowing how hard it is sometimes just to get out of bed in the morning. At an age when most men have long since retired, resting on their laurels, or have given up and become passive or cynical, my father is still passionate and involved.

These stories are also a tribute to my mother, Bettine, who fell in love with Dad, and he with her, when they were sixteen. That was sixty years ago. I am moved by my mother's steadfastness, by her fierce loyalty and love. I think of the two of them in their beloved Wyoming. Dad speeding to a house call across the wide-open spaces, his dogs on the seat beside him, Italian opera blaring out the windows, startling whole herds of antelope (or maybe they are used to it by now). And Mom caring for her Icelandic horses, walking with her dogs across the vast hay fields, or quietly reading, surrounded by her remarkable library—a woman passionately devoted to her husband, her family, and her friends.

Love is expressed in many ways. . . .

These stories are just a small sampling of the exceptional life of an exceptional man who happens to be my dad. I present them to you, dear reader, with a full and grateful heart.

GLENN CLOSE
Westchester County, New York

PART ONE

New York City

1947–1960

Introduction to New York

On June 7, 1951, my twenty-seventh birthday, I graduated from Columbia College of Physicians and Surgeons in New York City. My wife, Bettine, and our two girls came to the ceremonies on the steps of the university's Wilder Library. Tina was six, Glennie four. They had on little white dresses with red and blue trim and looked adorable.

I felt wonderful sitting between Tine and the girls, waiting for the walk to the podium to receive my degree of doctor of medicine. Tine had given me a family-seal ring with our initials and the date engraved on the inside as a birthday and graduation present. Under the Close family crest, which had come across the Atlantic with our ancestors from Yorkshire twelve generations ago, the family motto was inscribed: *Fortis et Fidelis*—Strong and Faithful. My father had worn a similar ring, and as I looked at mine, I thought of the first time he had let me accompany him to the American Hospital in Paris where he was the managing governor.

I think I was seven when the head nurse, Miss Compte, took my hand and led me on a tour of the hospital. She had brown eyes and a comforting smile, and her starched white apron rustled when she walked. My stomach was tight with anticipation as we stepped out of the elevator onto the surgical floor. Two large doors swung open and tall figures wearing white hats and long white gowns emerged, smiled at us, and walked down the immaculate corridor. I caught the whiff of ether and clean linen. Miss Compte eased the door open just enough for

3

me to peek through. Two gowned figures leaned over a stretcher outside one of the operating rooms. To my relief she explained that we could not go in because we were not properly dressed.

Before the Second World War, those operating rooms were used by some of the surgical giants of Europe. Dr. de Martel, called "The Magician," was one of the pioneers of modern neurosurgery; Dr. Chevalier Jackson looked into people's lungs with the bronchoscope he invented; Dr. Leriche, who discovered that an inability to achieve an erection was sometimes due to hardening of the arteries (known as the Leriche syndrome), used those operating rooms to perfect his procedure of stripping the nerves from the walls of arteries so they could expand and carry blood to where it was needed.

The surgical gowns, caps, and masks were like mystical robes of high priests, and the rubber gloves suggested exploring fingers capable of delicate maneuvers. But more than anything else the sound of starched linen and the faint smell of ether stimulated my imagination.

Downstairs in my father's office I told his secretary that I would be a surgeon when I grew up, and if I wasn't smart enough to be a surgeon, I'd be a hospital administrator like my father. She thought that was cute, but I was serious. I wanted desperately to be part of that mysterious world, to share in the prestige of being called "Doctor" and wear the proud uniform of a surgeon.

In 1942, I graduated a year ahead of my class at St. Paul's School and became a freshman at Harvard eager to pursue my goal. However, as I launched into my premed studies, my surgical sights were diverted by the girl I'd fallen in love with and the excitement of enlisting to fly in the Army Air Corps. Tine, my wife of fifty-seven years, and I were married when we were eighteen. Our individual goals to help people brought us together.

During my pilot training, Tine lived in boarding-houses and hotels next to training bases in Texas. At that time aviation cadets were allowed to be married but their wives were not recognized. After pilot training in Texas, I boarded a ship, sailed across the Atlantic, and was assigned to fly C-47s in a troop-carrier squadron stationed in Normandy a few weeks after the invasion. Our first daughter was conceived in New York the night before I boarded a troop ship for Europe. I saw her for the first time a year and three months later when I returned to the States. She was six months old and chewing on her crib.

My grades at Harvard were too low for admission to any medical school. I attended Columbia night school to correct that deficiency, and in 1947, I was accepted to Columbia College of Physicians and Surgeons. I am sure the letter that Tine's father, a respected industrialist, sent to the dean of admissions played a major part in my acceptance. He wrote:

> *My son-in-law wants to become a doctor. Personally I have no use whatsoever for the profession. However, his determination is such that I imagine he will make a good physician.*
>
> > *Sincerely,*
> > *Charles A. Moore*

Finally, I was launched toward the operating room of my dreams. I went through medical school on the GI Bill of Rights, supplemented by a home given to us by my father-in-law.

CHAPTER 1

The Cider Man

I MADE A LITTLE EXTRA MONEY at two part-time jobs during my years at Columbia College of Physicans and Surgeons. One was working in the blood bank at night. The other was collecting urine for a professor of endocrinology—a gland professor—who was doing research on postmenopausal gonadotropins. Gonadotropins are hormones that stimulate the gonads—the sex organs. I didn't know anything about gonadotropins at the time. All I knew was that the professor needed vast quantities of urine from old women who had gone through menopause and that he was willing to pay for a steady supply of it. I went to his small lab on the upper floor of the medical-school building to apply for the job. I knocked on the door and walked in after hearing a muffled "Come" from inside the lab.

The room was almost completely occupied by vats of boiling yellow liquid whose steam went through spirals of glass tubing and ended up, drop by drop, in a small glass beaker. The air was heavy and damp with the sweet but slightly ammoniacal smell of urine steam that escaped in little puffs from various rubber connections and corks in the apparatus. A small window was opened a crack and showed ice floes on the Hudson River below a sliver of the George Washington Bridge with its traffic in and out of New Jersey in the distance. The center of the window was wet, but at the edges delicate yellow crystals covered the window frame and reminded me that Christmas was around the corner.

"Good morning, sir," I said, looking for the professor.

"Good morning," came the reply from behind a wall of apparatus.

I saw, distorted by the vat, a wide pumpkin face grinning at me. The professor came out from behind the boiling liquid and shook hands. He was a small, normally proportioned man, with a ring of undisciplined, white hair framing a shiny, bald pate. Behind his thick gold-rimmed spectacles, which were partly covered by bushy white eyebrows, his bright blue eyes were energetic and filled with humor. He wore a light blue turtleneck sweater under a long open white lab coat that needed a trip to the laundry.

"Good morning, sir," I repeated. "I saw the notice you put on the bulletin board in the students' locker room about wanting urine. I would like to apply for the job. My name's Close, Bill Close, sir."

"Very good. Very good indeed, Close. Please sit down. You're the only student that's applied so far."

We sat on wooden stools surrounded by simmering urine emitting irregular blub-blubs as the aromatic gases struggled to the surface and released their vapors into the distilling tubes.

I remarked, "You seem to have plenty of urine, sir."

"Only for another week, then the supply will dry up. I've been getting it off the wards here at the center, but there have been complaints about my assistant walking through the hospital with jugs of urine, so I have to find another source." He spoke with the patience of a scientist dealing with an unappreciative lay public.

"Do you have any leads as to where you can get the stuff?" I asked, amused that there should be logistical problems associated with urine gathering.

"Yes, indeed, Mr. Close." He went over to an old metal desk covered with stacks of files and papers of various kinds and colors. He lifted one of the piles of documents and pulled out a piece of yellow foolscap.

"Here we are." He came back to his stool and handed me the piece of paper. On it was written:

Miss Ruby Rutledge, RN, Administrator
Presbyterian Home for Women
East Bronx, New York

"I haven't met this lady, but Dr. Hartright Place, one of our attendings in internal medicine, makes rounds in the home and has told the administrator that someone from this department would call on her to enlist her help with an important scientific research project." He waited for my reaction with a Cheshire-cat grin.

"You want me to go to the home and do that?"

"The sooner the better. I don't want to run out."

"What do I say to her? I'm afraid I don't really know what gonadotropins are or what they do."

"It's not all that complicated," said the professor. "Gonad comes from the Greek *gonos* meaning 'genitals.' Tropin comes from the Greek *tropos* meaning 'turn,' that is, turning on in response to a specific stimulus. In this case, in response to a lack of estrogen, secondary to the menopause. The Graafian follicle, named after Renier de Graaf, a Dutch anatomist in the eighteenth century . . ."

I was lost. I had come nowhere near the gonads on my cadaver in the anatomy lab. But I listened until he was through, making a few notes along the way.

"So," he concluded, "all you have to do is to go and see the lady on the paper and tell her that the cooperation of her older charges would be much appreciated. Okay?"

"I will certainly try, sir." I paused. "How much are you paying, sir?"

"Five dollars for a five-gallon jug. I'll throw in the alcohol and ether we use as a preservative."

"Do you know where this home is?" I asked.

"Across the Spidendival Bridge."

"That's on my way home."

"Good. Well, good luck, Close. I'm counting on you."
We got up and shook hands. I left him to his bubbling
vats, feeling that I might have bitten off more than I could
chew, so to speak.

On the next Friday I left school a little early after
spending an hour in the library looking up gonadotropins
and committing a short definition to memory.

I had made an appointment with Miss Rutledge
through her secretary, saying that I was a medical student
at the Columbia College of Physicians and Surgeons
involved in a research project that involved ladies "of a
certain age," as they say in France. The secretary had been
a little mystified by the request but had fixed the
appointment right away. A male medical student within
the halls of the ladies' home probably didn't happen
every day.

By leaving the medical center during the middle of the
afternoon, I avoided the weekend traffic. It was a cold day
and the gray slush along the West Side Drive was frozen
and rough. We had an old gray Nash at the time that had
well over a hundred thousand miles on it. The front seats
went all the way back and the whole car could be turned
into a big bed. Tine and I had crossed the country several
times when we had come home on leave from my Army
Air Corps cadet training in Texas. I drove onto the
Spidendival Bridge and paid a dime to the tollgate
attendant at the far end. What a miserable job he had.
Head and shoulders and right hand freezing as he stuck
them out over and over to collect dimes.

I found the exit off the parkway that led to the street,
two blocks west, where the home was. The area was a
pleasant residential one, with old houses, neat yards, and

big trees not yet replaced by high-rise apartment buildings. I drew up to a large, four-story, redbrick building with a glass-covered portico supported by filigreed iron columns protecting massive front doors. I parked in the driveway and got out of the car. I had on a gray pinstripe suit and my old Harrovian tie, dark blue with two white stripes, for the occasion. The house must have belonged to a wealthy family back in the days when this was countryside, with cows and sheep grazing, and Dutchmen smoking long clay pipes. The side of the building had two black, metal fire escapes zigzagging up to the flat crenellated roof. A fat gray squirrel bobbled across the crust of snow that covered the lawn and climbed up the first few feet of a large bare chestnut tree. I walked up the two steps to the front door. A small white enamel sign told me, in Gothic print, to PLEASE ENTER. I did, and found myself in a large foyer with a marble floor, heavy dark furniture, and a dark wood staircase covered with red carpet leading to the upper floors. The staircase had one of those rounded banisters that would have been fun to slide down. To the right of the entrance a modern-looking elevator waited for customers; the left side of the entrance hall was filled with a reception desk. Another little white enamel sign instructed me, also in Gothic script, to please ring. I tapped the bell, and a young woman appeared from an inner office.

"Good afternoon. I'm Mr. Close. I have an appointment to see Miss Rutledge."

"I'm Miss Feathertouch, Miss Rutledge's secretary. I spoke to you yesterday," said the young woman with a smile. She lifted the end of the reception desk and came into the hall. "Please follow me. Miss Rutledge is expecting you."

The clicking of her high heels echoed off the marble floor. She had on a dark blue skirt that swayed nicely with the movement of her buttocks. If her hair had been less severe and the hems of her stockings straight, she would have been attractive. She opened a paneled door and announced, "Mr. Close to see you." I walked into the room as the door closed behind me.

Miss Ruby Rutledge, RN, Administrator of the Presbyterian Home for Women, stood up from behind a large dark mahogany desk and came around to greet me. We shook hands. "How do you do, Doctor. Please sit down," she said, indicating a straight-backed chair next to the desk.

There were some letters in the "out" box; the "in" box was empty. Her typed schedule for the day and a pair of gold-rimmed glasses lay before her, otherwise the desktop was bare. Behind her, under the windows, was a bookcase containing the works of Shakespeare, bound in red leather with gold lettering, several dictionaries, a *Roget's Thesaurus* next to a large Bible in black leather, and a Presbyterian prayer book.

Four narrow Gothic windows behind Miss Rutledge let the gray winter light into the room. Her white hair was pulled to the back of her head in a bun that peeked out from behind her neck. Her face was composed and symmetrical like the farmer's wife in Grant Wood's *American Gothic*. She wore a blue serge tailored suit with a white blouse buttoned high. A simple lace collar covered the space between her Adam's apple and a strong chin, and a small, plain wooden cross on a fine gold necklace rested between her large, well-supported breasts. She looked kind, in a no-nonsense way. Formal, but not formidable. I guessed her age to be over sixty.

"Thank you for receiving me, Miss Rutledge," I said.

"My pleasure, Doctor," she said.

"I'm not a doctor yet," I volunteered. "I still have three years to go." She ignored the remark.

"How may we help you with your research?" she said getting right to the point.

"Miss Rutledge, I'm here on behalf of Professor Enright of the Department of Endocrinology at Columbia. He is doing important research on postmenopausal gonadotropins. Since you are a registered nurse, I am sure you know about gonadotropins," I said hopefully.

"I know nothing about gonadotropins. I did my nursing many years ago when oatmeal baths and flaxseed poultices were common treatments. As administrator, I have not had the time to keep up with all the medical developments. I would be most interested and grateful if you would tell me more, Mr. . . . " she put on her glasses and looked at her schedule sheet, "Close."

"Gonadotropins are hormones that stimulate the gonads, you know, the ovaries and testicles."

"I am quite aware of what the gonads are, Mr. Close."

"Well, as people get older their gonads don't work as well as they did when they were younger."

Her eyebrows went up ever so slightly. She was looking at me straight on. I cleared my throat and forged ahead.

"There are two gonad-stimulating hormones in women. One stimulates the follicles in the ovary to become little nests in which an egg can hatch. After the egg has left the nest, the other hormone stimulates the empty nest to produce the hormone that causes women to have a period."

"You are speaking of estrogen and progesterone, I presume."

"Yes, ma'am." The old RN knew more than she admitted.

"As we get older our gonads wear out."

"There is no need to belabor the point, Mr. Close."

"Oh, yes. Sorry. As the gonads wear out there is an increase in the amount of the two stimulating hormones.

It's as if a football team was getting more and more tired and making fewer and fewer touchdowns. So there are more and more coaches on the sidelines shouting stimulating things to the players, like, 'Come on, get off your . . . get off the grass and go, go, go.' But the players are too tired and worn-out to go, go, go. But the coaches don't give up. They continue to shout. They continue to try and stimulate the players. You know, the ovaries. See what I mean?"

Miss Rutledge smiled. "An interesting, if mixed, metaphor, Mr. Close. Your own?" she asked.

"Yes, I was listening to the Columbia football game on the way here."

"They would seem to need some gonadotropins, wouldn't you say?" said Miss Rutledge.

"That's right." I laughed. I was beginning to like this lady, as well as respect her.

Encouraged, I went on. "Professor Enright is trying to measure exactly how much the gonadotropins go up after the menopause."

"Why?" she asked.

"I'm not really sure about that, Miss Rutledge. But I think it's because the rise in the gonad-stimulating hormones, in the face of a decrease in gonadal function, may be a way to signal the end of the menopause."

"And the beginning of dilapidation," she added wistfully, fingering her wooden cross.

"The other reason is that there may be a connection between an increase in gonadotropins and hot flashes." I felt I was gazing at some horizon of research.

"We are all well beyond hot flashes here, Mr. Close. So, how can we help you?"

"The best way we have to measure gonadotropins in postmenopausal women is to extract the hormones from the ladies' urine."

"I see. That should not be a major problem. The ladies could supply urine samples, I suppose."

"We need much more than samples," I said. "We need large quantities of urine. It takes huge quantities of urine to extract tiny amounts of the hormones. The professor needs hundreds of gallons of urine."

"And how do you propose getting hundreds of gallons of urine?" she asked.

I decided to lay it all on the line. "We have these five-gallon jugs I could put in the ladies' bathroom, and we could get them to pee into the jugs—through a funnel, of course. I would do all the work of bringing the jugs and putting them in the bathroom and returning to get them. There would be no extra work for your staff."

"I see." There was a long pause. "It might give our ladies something to think about beyond their painful joints and disabilities. Would you come and talk to them if I get some of the livelier ones together?"

"Sure, Miss Rutledge. Anytime."

"Fine. I will have to speak to our executive committee, then I will call you to fix a time when you can give a little talk to the ladies and let them know that they are participating in medical research. I think they will like that." She got up and came around the desk. I stood. As we shook hands she asked, "What part do you play in this research, Mr. Close?"

"I get five dollars for each jug, Miss Rutledge."

"Good," she said, going to the door. "I think we can work things out."

"Thank you and good-bye, Miss Rutledge."

Miss Feathertouch clicked toward me from her office, smiled, and led me to the front door. I noticed that she had straightened the seams on her stockings.

"Have a good weekend, Doctor," she said, smiling broadly. "And come again."

Two weeks later, after tea and cookies, I gave a little talk to around twenty ladies about the importance of medical research and the complexities of biochemical extraction of hormones. Miss Rutledge and Miss Feathertouch stood in the back. Clearly some of the ladies didn't grasp what I was saying and several nodded off to sleep in their wheelchairs. The mention of sex, as in "sex hormones," however, opened a few eyes.

After the meeting, Miss Rutledge and I went back to her office and made the final arrangements. She escorted me up to the third floor in the elevator, and showed me a large toilet room in which there were four sinks and four toilet cabinets without doors. She said that if I came between the hours of four and five in the afternoon, each Friday, I could collect the jugs and put in fresh ones. The ladies had agreed that they would not go to the toilets during that time.

On the slow ride down to the front hall, Miss Rutledge said, "The executive committee thought that carrying jugs of urine through the front hall would be unseemly. I told them you would use the fire escape, which, as you may have noticed, goes right by the toilet-room window." I agreed. "And after your talk, Mr. Close, the ladies got together and decided to call you the 'Cider Man' rather than the 'Urine Man.' "

I laughed. "That was very nice of them."

The next Friday I started the weekly exercise of carrying four empty jugs up and four full jugs down the icy fire escape of the Presbyterian Home for Women.

The full jugs spent the weekends in the back of the Nash. The small amount of alcohol and ether we used as preservatives also kept the urine from freezing. Professor Enright was delighted with the steady supply of urine for his work, and I was delighted to make twenty dollars a week so easily.

Through the rest of the winter and into the spring, the excursions to the ladies' home became as routine as filling my car with gas. Then, on a hot summer evening, I was rushing to reach the home before four P.M. The four jugs were on the backseat of the car, the alcohol and ether sloshing around as usual. I was driving quite fast as I came up to the tollgate on the bridge, and as I braked to a stop a jug rolled off the seat and exploded, scaring the hell out of me and throwing glass all over the inside of the car. The cops dived into their booths, and resurfaced, pointing guns at me.

Shaken to the core, I said, "I don't have a gun. There was an explosion in the back of the car."

"Waddaya mean?" said the cop nearest to me.

"Well, I have a job collecting urine from the old ladies' home across the river, and—"

"Oh, yeah," he interrupted. "Don't move, mister."

It took half an hour to convince them that the explosion had been caused by the vaporization of the ether-alcohol mixture in the jugs and that, above all, I wasn't some sort of pervert.

Anyway, medical school was tough, but I got through and was accepted to the three surgical internship programs I had hoped for. The one I wanted the most was at Roosevelt Hospital in New York City.

Miss Rutledge came to my graduation.

CHAPTER 2

A Bedside Professor

KNOWLEDGE WITHOUT SENSITIVITY is best applied in a lab if coworkers can put up with it. Knowledge combined with humanity belongs at the bedside. One of my great teachers, Robert Loeb, Professor of Medicine at Columbia, demonstrated that quite naturally during his teaching rounds on the wards.

A classmate during our fourth year in school with a photographic memory and brains spilling out of his ears was presenting a patient to Dr. Loeb. I've forgotten the disease under review but remember it was fatal. Following the presentation we retreated to the conference room to discuss the patient and his future. Dr. Loeb turned to the student. "That was an excellent presentation of a disease which, unfortunately, we all know is incurable. When you go back to the bedside, the patient will want confirmation about his prognosis and what can be done for him. What is the first thing you would say to him?"

The student pondered a moment and, almost as a pre-thought, said, "Well, of course, I'd tell him not to worry, then . . . "

"What was that?" asked Loeb.

"I'd tell him not to worry."

"That," thundered the professor, "is the worst answer I have ever had to any question I have ever asked. In fact it is so bad that you will have to repeat your last year in this school." The student stood stunned and silent. "Now," said Loeb gently, "if I told you not to worry, would that help?"

On another occasion, I stood at the periphery of a large gathering of visiting professors, savants from overseas and house staff, as the brilliant, self-assured chief resident, Dr. Fein, bulging with knowledge and familiar with current international literature, prepared to present a patient with Addison's disease, one of Dr. Loeb's fortes.

Dr. Loeb approached the patient, greeted him by name, and shook hands saying a few words which seemed to relax him and make him smile. But the patient, clearly uncomfortable trapped in bed with the semicircle of people gazing at him, pulled at his covers and tried to fix his pillows. Once more, Dr. Loeb offered the patient his hand and helped him out of bed into a chair saying, "I think you will be more comfortable if your bed is made properly. Dr. Fein, please attend to it."

Fein fussed around a bit but was clearly out of his depth. He had no idea how to make a hospital bed with square corners and a tight bottom sheet. Dr. Loeb nodded to the head nurse who stepped forward and demonstrated the technique as she would to a fresh, eager candy striper. Dr. Loeb thanked her and the teaching continued with Fein just as brilliant but not quite as cocky.

CHAPTER 3

Grand Rounds

IN 1951, during my last year as a medical student, I served as an "extern" at Roosevelt Hospital, which covered the docks, Times Square, and what at the time we called "the Puerto Rican district." From the first day I walked up to the surgical floor in my clean white jacket, shirt, and tie and introduced myself to the head nurse, I wanted, more than anything else, to be part of that service.

As soon as I had a free moment, I rode up to the operating room floor and stepped into a glassed-in observation gallery to gaze in awe at the scene below. In the glare of a shadowless, pitiless light, a circle of people, gowned and masked, surrounded a patch of yellow skin framed by green towels. For a moment that solitary spot was unattached to a body, unrelated to the human hidden under the drapes. The nurse-anesthetist adjusted her machines and nodded. The instrument nurse handed the surgeon a scalpel, and instantly the initial incision became two fine red lines separating a narrow ellipse. Bright red beads glistened on the lips of the wound. The assistant sponged the blood with gauze. The spell was broken, the body invaded, the bleeders clamped and tied.

Later in my externship, when I was permitted to assist in the OR, I experienced the urgent drama of a dropping pressure and speeding pulse as a patient's life hovered on the brink of extinction. I heard the surgeon snap orders against a background of hissing, pulsating equipment as he enlarged the wound to expose and clamp an errant bleeder. I felt relieved as the pressure stabilized and the operation could resume.

19

As a third and sometimes a second assistant, I shared in the fatigue after hours of focusing my attention on the wound while pulling on a retractor. When my fingers became numb and shoulders ached and pleaded for relief, I persevered and, taking a deep breath, envied the surgeon who could move and change his position. "Someday . . ." I said to myself, "someday it will be my turn to operate."

I loved the operating room—the clean cotton smell of the mask, the smooth quiet ritual at the table between the nurse and the surgeon. The instruments were named for pioneers in surgery—Halsted, Kelly, Metzenbaum—and it seemed a privilege to use each for its own particular function. I wanted to be a surgical intern at the Roosevelt in the worst way.

As a fourth-year medical student, I received a lot of my training from the head nurse. I learned about nasogastric tubes and how to unplug them and keep them sucking out gastric and intestinal juices from guts plugged by twists or tumors. I changed purulent dressings and colostomy bags, rubbed sore, tired backs with alcohol, and gently soothed the skin with talc. Having worked as a volunteer night orderly at Mass General when I was in premed at Harvard, I was handy with a razor for surgical preps on patients scheduled for the OR. I could balance several bedpans at a time, when necessary. I drew blood, catheterized bladders, and gave enemas without messing up the patient or the bed. The head nurse was a statuesque blonde called "Mangey" by the residents, but Miss Mangleson by the rest of us. She was a stickler for detail, and she taught me to clean up my own mess when I forgot to check the sterilizer and reduced my share of rubber tubes to carbon.

I spent many hours sitting with patients at night. I heard, in their whispers and sleepless sighs, the hollow sounds of pain and fear of the unknown void beyond.

When death claimed one of them, I redoubled my efforts to learn more and work harder. Death was defeat and my aim was victory.

After a few weeks, I started to bug Dr. Tilney, the chief resident, to let me present a patient at Grand Rounds, in those days a very formal starched-white-uniform affair. He reminded me several times that I was a medical student and told me to cool it. I persisted. I did as much of his scut work as I could, cleaned up the messes he made when he wrapped plaster around broken limbs, and brought him cups of coffee when he was droopier than usual. I saw signs that my enthusiasm was wearing him down. He said, "Yes, yes," more often than, "No!" Finally, with a big sigh, he agreed that if a patient came into the accident room the next time our division was admitting, he would let me present the patient at Grand Rounds. "But you'll have to keep it short. Now quit pestering me." I quickly agreed to both requests.

That night a young ballerina from the Ice Capades, playing next door at Madison Square Garden, came in with a trimalleolar fracture of the ankle. My tall saturnine resident reduced the fracture dislocation in the accident room but decided that the injury needed to be stabilized. So we took the young woman upstairs to the operating room in the middle of the night and the necessary internal fixation with a wood screw was performed.

The next morning, Grand Rounds!!

There she was, "my" patient, propped up in bed, her injured leg on cushions, her shoulders snuggled in a little pink lacy bed jacket. Her cupid smile was etched in cherry red and her pretty face framed by blond hair falling to her shoulders. As the professors and house staff made a formal semicircle at the foot of her bed, Dr. Tilney rasped into my ear, "Make it short, Close." Movement ceased and the tall distinguished professor of surgery, Dr. "Pappy"

White, raised his eyebrows.

"Yes, Mr. Close."

I took a deep breath and froze—memory a blank—then blurted out. "This eighteen-year-old ballerina from the Ice Capades came into the accident room last night with a trimalleolar fracture of her ankle. Dr. Tilney reduced the dislocation, but because of the inherent instability of the injury, we took her up to the operating room and screwed her."

After a moment of stunned silence, pandemonium broke out—the patient joining in the laughter, thank God. The head nurse stiffened her spine and glared at me over her glasses. Dr. White raised his hand for order, then looked down at me. "Mr. Close, are you bucking for a job at this hospital?"

"Yes, sir," I replied.

"You've got it," he said.

CHAPTER 4

Answer Promptly

IREMEMBER my first night on call at Roosevelt Hospital. I had unpacked my books, put Tine's picture on the bedside table, and hung my clothes in the closet of the room assigned to me in the house staff quarters. It was a small room with a view of sooty roofs and red-brick walls. Two fat gray pigeons had been cooing on the windowsill, and the steam radiator hissed and knocked in the corner next to a tiled bathroom. A black telephone, which over the next few years became my Caligula, stood on the bedside table in front of Tine's picture. A small white desk and a wooden chair completed the furnishings.

House staff lived in the house. I suppose that was why they were called interns and residents in the first place. We were on duty every day and every other night. We had alternating Saturdays and Sundays off. On most days, when I was off for the night, I finished my work on the wards at five or six and then drove out to Connecticut to be with Tine and the children or, more realistically, to eat and sleep. I had to leave home before dawn the next morning to be back in midtown New York in time for the morning operating schedule.

On that first day, I met my resident and the other interns, and was assigned to a ward and patients. That night our division was admitting, so I was on duty. After stepping into a new uniform, I rode the elevator up to the surgical floor to chat with a few of the patients and go over their charts, then down to the cafeteria for coffee and a cigarette. I strolled over to the accident room and observation ward, ready for action, but everything was quiet. I stopped at the bank of pay telephones in the large waiting room across the hall from the admitting offices and called Tine.

"Hi, sweetheart. How's it going at home?"

"Fine. The girls are in bed reading, the dogs are fed, and Sandy's here in the kitchen. He still has diarrhea. I'm getting some rice water into him. Dr. Freddie said there was a bug around town. I wonder if he ever makes any other diagnosis?" Dr. Freddie Close was a very distant cousin and our trusted pediatrician.

"I guess a one-year-old has to make his peace with all sorts of germs," I replied.

"What are you up to?" she asked.

"I am on call; our division is admitting," I replied in measured tones—serious, on-the-ball tones like, "I am on standby in the ready room with my parachute strapped on, prepared to scramble when the horn goes off." All of a sudden, I heard the nasal twang of a telephone operator calling, "Dr. Close, Dr. Close, answer promptly!" over the pager. "Answer promptly" was the code for an emergency. Oh, my God, I thought, I have arrived, this is it. I have an emergency!

"I have to go!" I shouted into the phone, and slammed it down without saying "I love you," or even good-bye. I heard about it the next time I was home, but at that moment the scramble horn had gone off and I was being called to the colors, called into battle. My adrenals fired. I rushed to a hospital telephone and picked up the receiver. "This is Dr. Close."

"They want you in the operating room, Doctor."

"I'm on my way," I said, bugles sounding in my head. Holy Jesus, the operating room! I ran upstairs—couldn't wait for the elevator—and, flinging open the door, dashed down the hall toward the nurses' station.

The operating room was run by a very military female

called Miss Tausma. Everybody, except the interns, called her "Plasma." She was a shapely nurse with arched black eyebrows and a white turban covering her dark hair. Her green OR uniform fit her like a surgical glove. I came charging up to her desk. She looked up.

"Dr. Close?"

"Yes, ma'am."

"Get changed, quickly. You are needed in Major One," she commanded.

Major One! Fantastic! I rushed to the locker room, stripped off my whites. The first pair of scrub pants I put on were too big. I rummaged around on the shelf—couldn't go in there looking like a baggy medical intern. I pulled on the proper green pants, tightened the drawstring, and slipped an OR shirt over my head. I picked out a pressed green cap and, looking in the mirror, made sure the crease was centered on my forehead, like the garrison cap I had worn in the air corps. Sweating with excitement, I tied a mask around my neck and face and molded the metal strip to the shape of my nose. I ran out of the dressing room, down the hall, and into the scrub room for Major One.

Looking into the operating room through the glass in the door, I saw a large number of gowned and masked people gathered around the table, their heads bent forward and fixed in concentration. Sticking to the usual etiquette of those days, I poked my head into the room and said, "Sir. May I speak?"

Someone said, "Yeah."

"I'm Dr. Close."

"You the intern?"

"Yes, sir!"

"Okay, Close. Get scrubbed and come on in."

Never had hands been so carefully scrubbed, or nails picked so clean with a cherry stick. I stepped into the operating room and the sponge nurse (one of the sterile nurses) was holding a gown spread out. I plunged my arms into the sleeves one at a time, then dove my fingers into the rubber gloves she held open for me. She wrapped a towel over my hands and said, "Wait." I did, my heart pounding with anticipation. After five minutes, according to the clock on the wall, of just standing there, my outside pristine and sterile, my insides spring-tight like a racehorse at the gate, the senior surgeon turned around and looked at me.

"You the intern?" he asked again.

"Yes, sir!"

"Get under the table."

"What?"

"Please get under the table, Doctor. I am doing an all-American. The patient has cancer of the rectum and we are taking everything out. The pelvis is filled with tumor and adhesions, and I am having a hard time finding the rectum. Get under the table, put your finger in his anus, and wiggle it so I can feel where I am."

One of the unsterile, circulating nurses picked up the edge of the drapes with one hand and retrieved the towel off my hands with the other. She indicated the floor with her head and I crawled under the table. The patient was in the lithotomy position, that is, with his legs in stirrups. It was very crowded down there under the drapes with all sorts of feet covered with operating booties, table legs, foot pedal controls, wires, and tubes with stuff going in and other larger tubes with stuff coming out. It didn't smell very good. But after a little groping around, I finally found the patient's anus and stuck my thumb in it. I was abashed but did not admit it to myself.

"Are you in?" asked the surgeon from above, his voice was muffled.

"Yes, sir, I'm in."

"Wiggle your thumb."

I wiggled my thumb.

"Are you wiggling your thumb?"

"Yes, sir."

"I can't feel it. I guess we have a way to go. Hang in there, Doctor."

"Yes, sir." I pulled my leg up and rested my elbow on my kneecap to steady my thumb, which was getting warm in the anal canal.

"Clamp. Forceps. Scissors . . . no, give me the Metzenbaums. Sponge!" They were working down into the pelvis over my head.

I must have stayed under those drapes for half an hour with my thumb in the anal canal, sweating like a pig, until they found out where they were. When they finally had no need of my help, I was told I could leave. I crawled out and stretched my aching joints.

"Is that it, sir?" I asked.

"Yes," replied the surgeon. Then he turned and looked at me and smiled above his mask. "Thank you very much, Dr. Close, that was a big help."

CHAPTER 5

The Subway

ONE OF OUR FIRST DUTIES as interns was to ride the ambulance. A law had recently been passed to the effect that all death certificates had to be signed by a doctor; apparently, when the police sergeants in charge of the emergency squads had been responsible for certifying death, several of the "dead" had awakened in the icebox of the city morgue and caused embarrassment to the authorities. Thus, now, a doctor was required to pronounce dead the "jumpers" in front of subway trains or out of windows, and the "floaters," bloated and bobbing in the slimy water under riverside pilings. We interns also pronounced dead the winos in threadbare coats, crumpled and stiff against the cold steel supports of the elevated highway by the docks. Often, a clawlike hand with cracked dirty fingernails still clutched a bottle wrapped in a brown paper bag. We signed the death certificates of murder victims. Sometimes we signed out an old man whose heart had failed in the act of screwing a whore in a flophouse off Times Square. It tore at my guts to acknowledge death in children, often waifs beaten and torn, or emaciated and dead in their own filth from disease and malnutrition. We had a police ambulance service with the Nineteenth Precinct. A red phone in the emergency room provided a direct line to the station. They needed us as much as we needed them.

"Mad Mike" McGonchy was one of our ambulance drivers. I found out, after the first few rides in the back of his ambulance, that he was the reason they took the sirens off the city ambulances for a while. Mad Mike's style was full speed ahead, down the wrong side of the street, up on the sidewalk, with the siren going full blast. Those riding in the back put pillows against the bulkhead and assumed the position called by the crews of England's Royal Air Force "Dingy, dingy, prepare for ditching." McGonchy wrecked ambulances.

One evening when I was too exhausted to drive home on my night off, I had just crawled into bed when the phone rang.

It was "Ma" Ware, the hospital operator. "The intern on ambulance call is out delivering a baby for the Puerto Ricans and another call just came in on a jumper in the subway."

"You must be kidding," I replied.

"I do not kid about emergencies, dear."

"Okay, okay, I'll be right there," I said, hanging up. Ma Ware had been at the hospital switchboard since Bell had invented his infernal machine. No nook or cranny was protected from her paging and telephone calls. From her basement office, she supported the hospital like a hidden girder.

Pulling on the soiled uniform I had thrown into the laundry basket, I staggered downstairs and along the corridor that led from the residents' quarters to the hospital. The ambulance was warming up, its rear end over the sidewalk in front of the accident room, its doors open. McGonchy was driving. Taking the pillows off the stretcher, I sat against the bulkhead and stuffed them behind me. Mario, the ambulance attendant, came out of the accident room and tossed the emergency bag onto the stretcher.

"Ya look comfortable, Doc," he said, laughing as he closed the back doors. He climbed into the front seat next to McGonchy.

We charged into the traffic of Eighth Avenue with the

siren screaming and swerved onto Forty-ninth Street, heading for the IRT subway station only a few blocks away. Three police cars had pulled up to block the narrow stairway leading to the trains. Their flashing lights swept across the entrance to the underground tunnels and picked out cops keeping the curious at bay. McGonchy pulled up. Mario jumped out; I handed him the bag and climbed out myself, wide-awake and filled with apprehension as the siren's echo died in the street.

I followed Mario down the stairs to the station platform, where the transit police pushed back onlookers to let us through. Beyond the low muttering of the crowd and shuffling of feet, a train whistle sounded hollow in a distant tunnel. I glanced at the rails. The driver had backed the train away from the body of a man lying prone across the tracks, his legs and arms splayed out unnaturally. A shabby brown jacket, its lining ripped into shreds, was hiked up over his shoulders, hiding his head and neck. Pools of dark blood had formed in the crushed rock between the greasy ties. We made our way between the crowd and the edge of the platform to the end of the station. I climbed down a ladder and walked gingerly between the tracks toward the body, wondering if one of the gleaming steel rails was "hot."

My adrenaline surged when I heard the rumble of a train approaching behind me. I glanced over my shoulder and was relieved to see it pulling in slowly on the other track. It came to a halt with screeching brakes and I looked up to see faces pressed against the windows. They gawked down at me with the same look of sadistic gratification seen on the faces of ringside spectators when a fighter is pummeled to a pulpy mass by an opponent with a killer instinct. I stepped forward, making sure of my footing. Cigarette butts, old Kleenex, and a child's mitten lay on the dirty gravel between the ties. I glanced up at the platform: people jostled for a better look. I heard the doors close in the train on the other track and it moved slowly away. The ground and the body in front of me shook as the train pulled out. The jumper's feet were in the wrong position. His shirt was torn and soaked with blood from a large gash across his back. His upper chest was against the rail. I reached over and pulled the jacket away from his head. Icy claws gripped my stomach. The head had been severed from the neck and lay, facedown, in a large pool of congealing blood. A reflex—I reached for my stethoscope.

"Ya ain't gonna find a heartbeat with his head off, Doc," came from the platform.

"Oh. Oh, yes. Thank you," I said, glancing up. An older man looked down at me with sympathy. I felt like throwing up and dying at the same time as I turned around and walked back unsteadily to the ladder. Grabbing it, I held on tightly until the nausea and light-headedness left me. I looked up and saw McGonchy.

"C'mon Doc, yer okay," said McGonchy, reaching out to pull me up.

I scribbled a signature on the form the sergeant pushed at me, then followed my two ambulance men through the silent people. We passed the coroner's men coming down the stairs with a body bag on a stretcher. At the subway entrance, the crowd had wandered off and a single squad car remained. We climbed into the ambulance and started back to the hospital. McGonchy opened the sliding glass window that separated front from back.

"We're stoppin' at da Market Diner for coffee."

"Okay by me," said Mario, who had climbed into the back of the ambulance with me. I nodded.

The Market Diner was the eating place for our ambulance crews and the truck drivers who hauled freight to the docks. We sat at the counter, and the waitress, a synthetic redhead with a wide painted mouth, brought us coffee.

"You boys out on the town again?"

Mario smiled and slurped his coffee.

"Howya doin', babe?" said McGonchy. "Say, Myrt, warm up wunaya big bran muffins and pud lotsa budder on it for Doc here. He just done good." Myrtle raised her penciled eyebrows, gave me a motherly look, and put a muffin in the warmer.

"Thanks, McGonchy," I said. I felt a surge of warmth toward this veteran who had seen it all, but still had feelings for a novice.

CHAPTER 6

Maria

IT WAS VERY RARE that the intern on duty did not have at least two ambulance calls during the night. Most of them involved ferrying people from the street or a tenement to a hospital; some were DOAs. Our ambulance was frequently called to pick up women in labor who thought they were about to deliver. Many of the calls came from the Puerto Rican district. Anyone could put a dime in a telephone, call a special number, and get an ambulance to take them to a hospital. They even got their dime back.

More often than not a maternity run turned into a simple taxi service, but a doctor had to go along. There were the challenging times when he had to decide quickly whether there was time to transport the woman to a hospital, or whether he would have to deliver the baby in the tenement. Above all, the third alternative of having the baby in the ambulance was to be avoided since custom dictated that the doctor had to provide the driver and the attendant with a case of beer for cleaning up the mess. On the other hand, if the intern elected to deliver the baby at home, he and the crew might be stuck there for a while.

I never became competent at judging how long the end stages of labor would last before the moment of birth. In medical school, my training in obstetrics consisted of following the vital signs on a few mothers in labor and trying to hear fetal heartbeats. I learned the theory of various "presentations" but never delivered a baby. Once, I was handed a very slippery newborn when the resident needed to cut the cord wrapped around its neck. I was scared of dropping it and relieved when a nurse grabbed it by the heels and took over. Surgery, I loved in any form; I could operate on anything any time of the day or night. But in delivery rooms, my knees turned to Jell-O and my stomach rose to my throat. I have never understood why. Frankly, I have never tried to find out.

Not long after the subway accident, I was routed out of bed at 1:00 A.M. on a winter night for yet another maternity call. I put my old army coat over my uniform and walked down to the ambulance in the parking lot. McGonchy was driving again. He had the engine running, trying to warm up the inside. Walking on my toes to keep the gray snow out of my white shoes, I climbed into the back and flopped down on the stretcher, hoping for a little more sleep. I was very tired and annoyed at having to escort another pregnant woman to a hospital. Mario climbed in with the delivery bag and closed the doors. I sat up as we headed out into the city again with the siren screaming, even though, at that time of the night, there was little traffic on Eighth Avenue. In those days, New York City's West Side was quiet and relatively peaceful in the small hours of the morning. Empty streets slick with frost reflected cold light from occasional street lamps. Small plumes of steam rose from manhole covers and danced wildly when a taxi drove by on its way to the barn.

My body moved passively with the motion of the ambulance; I hoped that we could load the woman fast and drop her off at a city hospital. After a few minutes we pulled up to a tenement. The street was deserted. At the bottom of the stoop, refuse overflowed from garbage cans and mixed with the frozen slush on the sidewalk. The three of us trudged up the worn, slick steps.

I was glad to be sandwiched between McGonchy and Mario. I appreciated McGonchy's street wisdom. Although he was not a cop, he wore a cop's uniform with a hospital badge on his chest. He knew most of the policemen in the precinct, and had grown up with some of the older sergeants. His booming brogue could clear a path through a crowd. Mario was a quiet, huge man with soft brown eyes who chuckled at life, and worked overtime to buy a little house in Far Rockaway for his wife and seven-year-old daughter. Off duty, he painted houses. When he wasn't riding the "bus," he helped out in the accident room. Once, when I was about to be attacked by a huge, crazy man who wanted to escape from the hospital, Mario heard my shouts and, running into the room, wrestled the man to the floor. I never let a patient come between me and the door after that. Violent crime was endemic in our part of the city, but I felt safe walking into the tenement between the two veterans.

Through a cracked pane in the front door, I could see a dim light inside a narrow hallway and a steep staircase on the right. Usually the husband, or brother, or friend was at the entrance to meet the ambulance and lead us to the patient, but not this time.

McGonchy opened the door and yelled, "Ambulance!" No one appeared. He pulled out the dispatcher's slip and, holding it under the yellow bulb, read "fourth floor." The place was filthy and smelled of rancid lard and garlic.

As we reached the first floor the doors of the two rooms on the landing shut with a click; we continued climbing. At each level, doors were opened as far as the security chains would allow. After a brief scrutiny from those inside, the doors were closed and bolted. We were not here for them; it was none of their business.

On the third landing, we surprised two rats with their heads buried in a brown bag of stinking garbage. Coffee grounds, old orange skins, and pieces of rotting cabbage were scattered all over the floor. They scurried away with scraps in their mouths. McGonchy kicked at the bag and sat on the steps. Panting and snorting like a walrus, he took off his cap and wiped the sweat off his forehead and the top of his bald scalp. Mario and I waited for him to catch his breath. His beer belly and chronic cough were handicaps on tenement stairs.

"Whadda goddamn dump," he muttered, wiping the inside of his cap. He stood up and stuffed the handkerchief into his back pocket.

"You okay, McGonchy?" asked Mario.

"Sure, I'm okay. Where's the goddamn patient?"

The door on the right opened. A wizened Puerto Rican with a stubble of gray on his chin and rheumy eyes pointed upstairs.

"*Es Maria. Ariba las escalones, para la derecha,*" said the old man, pointing upstairs and to the right. "*Su hombre se ha ido*—Her man has gone away," he added with a shrug.

We stood in front of the door on the fourth floor.

"Go on in, Doc," said McGonchy.

I listened for a moment. "I think I hear a dog growling."

"Donworry abahdit," said Mario, knocking on the door and opening it. I followed cautiously. A dog snarled from under the bed, but stopped on a command from the young Puerto Rican woman lying on a double bed that almost filled the room. Two small children, their eyes big with wonder, sat cross-legged at the foot of her bed playing quietly with a rag doll and a cardboard box. I glanced around the room. A rusty radiator pinged and spat below a narrow, bare window next to the bed. Plastic cups and plates were neatly stacked next to an electric ring in an alcove to our right. The faded wallpaper was badly stained, and the ceiling plaster cracked where it met the walls. The room was steamy hot and smelled of bodies and cooking oil.

Mario grabbed my coat as I slipped it off. I looked at the girl—she seemed young enough to be called that. Her hands pressed on her bulging abdomen and her breathing came in small gasps for a moment, then subsided as the contraction eased. The single bulb hanging from the ceiling lit a small crucifix on the wall above her head. I approached the bed.

"Maria?"

"*Sí*" she nodded. "*Gracias por ver benido.*"

She was beautiful. A white T-shirt covered her breasts. Her shiny black hair fell to her shoulders; a tress stuck to her damp forehead. Long eyelashes cast shadows on her unblemished cheeks flushed from the efforts of labor. Her knees were flexed and a frayed towel covered her pelvis and upper thighs. The mattress was wet from the release of her waters and the pillow under her head was damp with sweat. Her expression was serene—untroubled by her surroundings.

I turned to Mario. "I'd better have a look."

He opened the OB bag and handed me sterile gloves. I pulled them on and sat on the edge of the bed. "I need to check the baby, and see how you're doing, Maria. Okay?" I asked.

"Ees okay," she replied.

I slipped my hand under the towel. I could feel the baby's head starting to crown. The young mother took a deep breath and tightened up. Her hands gripped her thighs and she pushed hard. I could feel the infant's head bulge out a little more.

Alarmed, I said, "We'll have to deliver her here, Mario. The baby's almost out." This was my first real delivery, and in a tenement where I could not get help. Mario dove into the bag and quickly laid out the drapes and instruments I would need.

The contraction released its hold on her uterus and

Maria closed her eyes and let out her breath slowly.

"Good, Maria. You're doing fine," I said nervously, trying to remember the course of events in labor.

She took my gloved hand and squeezed it. "Ees okay," she said, stating a fact. Suddenly I knew there was little I needed to do.

The contractions came rapidly, lasting a good minute—I sat there timing them. With my stethoscope I picked up the baby's heartbeat easily; it was strong and fast. I went over to the sink and ran cold water on a towel and wiped away the sweat from Maria's forehead and her face. She thanked me, and with each contraction she pushed harder, then relaxed as it waned and caught her breath before the next one came.

There were no sounds in the room except for her heavy breathing and the sputtering of the radiator as the labor progressed. The children at the foot of the bed sat quietly and looked away. After a long hard contraction, during which she pushed with all her might, she let out a soft cry and the baby came.

"A beautiful little boy, Maria."

She smiled and with a deep sigh let her body rest.

Lifting him from between her legs, I wrapped him in a sterile diaper from the kit. I sucked out his nose and mouth with a rubber bulb and he let out a cry and pinked up right away. After tying the cord and cutting it, I laid him in the comfortable groove between Maria's breast and her arm. She kissed the top of his head then closed her eyes.

The afterbirth came without trouble. Mario and I pulled the soiled sheet from under her, put fresh linen from the OB bag on the bed, and covered her with a half sheet.

The door opened a little. "You through in there?" asked McGonchy.

"Sure, we're coming," said Mario, packing up.

"You go ahead. I'll be right down," I said. Mario left and I heard him say, "Lez go. Doc'll be right down." Their footsteps faded down the stairs.

I looked down at the young mother. Her eyes were closed and the infant suckled gently at her breast. The two other children and the dog slept. I sat gently on the edge of the bed. Maria opened her eyes and turned to look at me.

I said slowly, "I will get the public health nurse to come and see you later today."

She nodded, but I was not sure she had understood.

"*Nurse, infermière*"—maybe the Spanish was like the French—"*elle viente* today. Okay?"

"*Comprendo,* Doctor. Nurse . . . come . . . today," she repeated.

"That's right, Maria," I said, laughing.

She smiled and held out her hand and I took it.

"*Gracias,* Doctor," she said, softly. "*Muchas gracias.*"

"Oh Maria, I did nothing. You did it all . . . so well." I held her hand and her warm brown eyes looked into mine.

The pale wash of a cold dawn was seeping into the room. I thought of all the blood and screaming and brutality I had seen over the past months. The woman covered with black fuzz from a cheap shag rug on the floor of the flophouse room where she had been raped and killed. The small scruffy boy with his hand, deformed and swollen, pressed against his narrow chest, pulled along to the nurses' station by an older sister in an unraveling sweater, too big for her thin little body. The "jumpers," and "floaters," and drunken bums without homes, without even filthy, sweaty rooms in a rat-infested tenement. We took care of them all as quickly and as efficiently as we could. The city paid. If they were interesting and operable, we kept them; if not, they were "shipped" to a city hospital—Roosevelt had that privilege. Action suppressed sentiment, but injured kids taking care of each other, and abandoned dogs, struck something deep inside me that hurt.

I got up quietly, put on my coat, and opened the door. I glanced back. Maria was looking at me.

"*Adios*, Doctor."

"*Adios*, Maria. *Muchas gracias*. Thanks for what you have given me." She lifted her hand from the baby's head, gave me a little wave, and smiled. I went out of the room and closed the door softly behind me.

CHAPTER 7

The Little Lady
in a Pillbox Hat

LITTLE CHILDREN fending for each other in a hostile world, or the older, gentler folk who came to New York's emergency rooms, were reminders that there was more to life than the miserable turmoil and blood and booze of the usual Friday nights.

On one such night, after finishing an admitting note on a patient, I headed for the operating room, where a woman, bleeding from the head, had just been put on the table. I paused in the hall as an orderly escorting a dignified, elderly lady passed on the way to one of the examining rooms. She looked out of place. I continued into the OR. The woman on the table was smashed on rotgut wine; the stink of her acrid breath filled the room. Her head was wrapped in a four-inch Ace covering a wad of gauze pads. Blood had soaked the dressing and stained the white sheet on the table. I removed the bandages, and blood spurted from a huge, scalping-type laceration running from ear to ear.

"What happened?" I asked Peggy Leggy, the accident-room nurse, who was trying to keep the woman from falling off the table.

"I don't know. She's too drunk to tell me. The ambulance picked her up on the street and brought her in," said Peg as the woman started to sit up.

"Lie down, lady. I've got to stop the bleeding from the top of your head," I said, pushing her down on the table.

"Who're you?" she asked, her red puffy eyes trying to focus.

41

"I'm the doctor. I have to sew you up or you'll bleed to death." Peggy and I pushed her shoulders to the table. The orderly had wrapped his arms around her knees and was lying across her lower body. He grunted every time she tried to kick him off.

"Fuck you, sonnovabish." She vomited all over Peggy, but we kept our grip. Her abuse of Peg, the hospital, and the world was vulgar and loud. Thick stinking spittle ran out of the corner of her mouth. What teeth she had were brown with rot. Her struggle to get up continued. My greens and the apron of Peg's uniform were covered with gore and vomit. We rolled her onto her stomach and strapped her to the table with rolls of four-inch adhesive. She fought and cursed and spit at us. I stuffed gauze pads into her mouth and went to work.

After clamping and tying the bigger bleeders, we shaved the wound edges and washed her head with soap and water. Peggy irrigated the grime and dried blood out of the wound with saline as I held the edges of the wound apart. The slash was razor straight and the skin edges needed no debriding. After tying off more bleeders, I sutured the scalp back onto its bed.

Now quiet, in a drunken stupor, we cut her loose from the table and heaved her onto a gurney. Peggy raised the side bars and wheeled her into the hall where she could be watched. The orderly returned to the OR with a mop and bucket. He swabbed the floor, sprayed the room with Lysol to get rid of the smell, and covered the table with a clean sheet. The room was now ready for the next one.

In the staff room, I washed up and changed into fresh greens. A medical intern was sleeping on the bench. Closing the door gently, I returned to the emergencies: back into the world of the docks, the Puerto Rican district, Times Square, and Madison Square Garden on a Friday night—vicious and violent. Thank God for the red phone to the Nineteenth Precinct.

Peggy held up an admitting slip, "Room four, Doctor. There's an elderly lady that needs to see you."

"Okay, what's she got?" I asked as we headed down the hall.

"I dunno. Says she doesn't feel well."

I opened the door for Peggy and we walked in. The furniture was spartan—a gurney against a wall, a stool, a small corner sink, and a white metal chair in the other corner. The concrete floor had a drain in the middle; heavy bars outside the windows prevented patients brought in by the police from escaping.

A little lady dressed in a sensible, tailored suit sat on the chair. A black velvet pillbox hat with a little veil perched on the top of her white hair. She appeared to be, as we say, "in no acute distress." I closed the door and sat on the stool. The quiet in the room was a relief.

"Good evening, ma'am. What can I do for you?" I asked.

She sat up a little straighter, "I don't know, Doctor. I don't feel ill, but then I don't feel normal either. I have never felt like this before and I do not know why."

"In what way do you not feel well?"

She paused, concentrated, and shook her head a little. "I just feel funny."

"You have been feeling funny for how long, ma'am?"

"Well," she answered, "I felt fine until after dinner."

I could hear a ruckus beyond the door as the orderlies tried to calm a woman who was screaming hysterically. The little lady raised her eyebrows and looked at the door. "It's okay, ma'am," I said. "They will not come in here."

Peggy, cuddling a clipboard against her chest, leaned against the gurney, rested her chin on the top of the board, and smiled. She had taken off her apron, but her uniform still showed signs of our last patient. Good nurses, like good crew chiefs and good sergeants, make the world go around.

There was a knock at the door and Mario peeked in. For a moment the noise of a siren winding down filled the room. "The scalp lady's ready ta go, Doc. Waddaya want we should do wid'er?"

"You really want to know?" Peggy gave me a look. "I'll check her before she leaves; it won't be long." We had to keep things moving on Friday nights. The door closed and the noise in the hall was muted. "Sorry about the interruption, ma'am." Then, with a conscious change of pace, I continued, "What did you have for dinner?" She settled into the chair with a little wiggle.

"We had a wonderful dinner. My son is an officer on the Queen Mary. She docked this evening and he called and invited me to dinner at the Waldorf-Astoria. We had such a good time. There was an orchestra playing dance music, and he was so well and happy. He is very handsome in his uniform, you know."

"I am sure he is. What did you eat?" I asked again.

Still slowly and deliberately, she replied. "Well, we started with oysters. Then lobster thermidor—I do love seafood, Doctor. He's an officer on the Queen Mary . . . Oh, but I told you that, didn't I?"

"Yes, ma'am, you did. What else did you have?"

Concentrating hard, she continued, "We had an ice cream and meringue dessert. It's called . . ." She paused.

"Baked Alaska?"

"That is right, Doctor. It was all very good."

Again Times Square was making a statement on the other side of the door, but I persisted, with a great sense of dedication to medical history. "Did you have anything else?"

She thought for a moment, then looked me straight on. "We had minty cream drinks in narrow crystal glasses as we sat listening to the music. They were delicious. A beautiful emerald green."

"Just one?" I asked.

"Two or three," she replied, raising her eyebrows and blinking her eyes quizzically.

"Well," I said, with a sigh of relief, "Miss Leggy will bring you a cup of coffee, and I'll be back in a while to see how you are doing. I think it is something we can look after." As we left the room and closed the door Peg and I turned to each other and said in unison, "Don't tell her she's drunk."

For half an hour I sutured and calmed and treated a world of misery and pain, then returned to Room 4 to check on the little lady with the pillbox hat. "How are you doing?"

"I feel perfectly fine," she said, with authority. "What do you think was the matter with me, Doctor?"

"Oh, it was probably the night air in New York. Sometimes it does not go too well with sweet emerald drinks in narrow crystal glasses."

She stood up, brushed invisible lint from her skirt, and said, "Thank you for your time, Doctor. I will be on my way now."

PART TWO
Africa

1960–1976

Introduction to Africa

I WAS STILL A SURGICAL RESIDENT at Roosevelt when Tine met members of a missionary organization called Moral Re-Armament (MRA). A couple came to the house and talked about their convictions.

At that time our marriage was under considerable stress. I was preoccupied with surgery; Tine was at home taking care of four small children. My work at the hospital was exciting and sometimes dramatic; her days were routine and repetitive. She craved adult conversation; I longed for sleep. My visits home were rare and short. Tine felt that if we both faced our natures squarely, and were honest with each other, our marriage might be saved.

What was MRA? The New Columbia Encyclopedia gives some historical facts about the founder of Moral Re-Armament:

> *Buchman, Frank Nathan Daniel 1878–1961, American evangelist, born Pennsburg, Pa. The international movement he founded has been variously called First Century Christian Fellowship, the Oxford Group, Moral Re-Armament (often known as MRA), and Buchmanism. Buchman was ordained in the Lutheran ministry in 1902. He was head (1905–15) of religious work at Pennsylvania State College. In 1921, Buchman, after five years of extension lecturing for the Hartford Theological Foundation, visited England. There he preached "world-changing through life-changing" among the students at Oxford, hence the name Oxford Group. In*

49

1938 he instituted a campaign known as Moral Re-Armament. The work of evangelism for personal and national spiritual reconstruction is conducted informally and intimately in groups gathered in educational institutions, in church congregations or in homes. "House parties" take the place of conferences, and religious experiences are shared in personal confessions. The evangelists stress absolute honesty, purity, love, and unselfishness.[1]

Another definition is taken from one of Frank Buchman's speeches, "What Are You Living For?" published in a book entitled *Remaking the World:*

Only the very selfish or the very blind person is content to leave the world as it is today. Most of us would like to change the world. The trouble is, too many of us want to do it our own way.

Some people have the right diagnosis, but they bring the wrong cure. They reckon without God and without a change in human nature, and the result is confusion, bitterness and war. Other people are quite sure they have the answer in theory, but they always want somebody else or some other nation to begin. The result is frustration and despair.

When the right diagnosis and the right cure come together, the result is a miracle. Human nature changes and human society changes.

Let me illustrate this with a personal word, because it happened to me one day forty-two years ago. For the first time I saw myself with all my pride, my selfishness, my failure and my sin. "I" was the center

1. "Buchman, Frank Nathan Daniel," *The New Columbia Encyclopedia* (New York: Columbia University Press, 1975), 386.

of my own life. If I was to be different, then that big "I" had to be crossed out.

I saw the resentments I had against six men standing out like tombstones in my heart.

I asked God to change me, and He told me to put things right with those six men. I obeyed God, and wrote six letters of apology.

That same day God used me to change another man's life. I saw that when I obeyed God, miracles happened. I learnt the truth that when man listens, God speaks; when man obeys, God acts; when men change, nations change.[2]

The challenge was heady wine at the beginning. Buchman's philosophy allowed me to straighten out a few personal "sins" and immediately jump into a world arena. Although my career in New York seemed assured—I would become the assistant of one of the senior surgeons at Roosevelt—the prospect of starting as junior attending in the varicose-vein clinic and struggling up the long, steep ladder of the hierarchy lacked excitement. In those days one could expect a real letdown during the transition from an overworked, responsible chief resident in surgery, to the low man on the attending surgeons' totem pole waiting for the crumbs to fall from the professors' tables. The prospect of a "world mission" that would change people and nations impelled me to resign from my surgical residency at Roosevelt six months early and commit to MRA full-time. Would it have been smarter to finish my residency and take my boards in surgery? Probably, and in fairness to MRA, some of its leaders

2. Frank Buchman, "What Are You Living For?" in *Remaking the World* (New York: R. M. McBride, 1949).

urged me to follow that course. But "singleness of purpose" and "boundless enthusiasm," labels pinned on me by my teachers in England, joined forces with the glorious feeling of being called and plugged my ears to appeals to good sense from my surgical mentors. These men were concerned and gracious enough to invite me to lunch at their clubs, where they tried to reason with my head. But my newly acquired religious fervor discouraged reasonable conversation. Neither what they said nor what they offered changed my mind about my new calling.

In 1954, Tine and I were invited to Caux, Moral Re-Armament's sumptuous headquarters in Switzerland. The day came, soon after that, when I squeezed my past, including my activities as squadron-morale-and-booze officer during the war, through MRA's moral wringers. I was pronounced ready to serve as a purified conduit between God and the world. Tine went through the same procedure. Freed from guilt and energized by self-righteousness, we sacrificed our personal ambitions and sexual drives to a noble cause. We were ready and eager to take on the rebuilding of the world through change in human nature. We committed our lives to God, to MRA, and to living by the Four Standards. We also committed a large sum of money.

MRA encouraged, actually demanded, that God's guidance be sought by writing down all thoughts in a little book during a period of meditation, usually upon awakening and having a cup of tea. These thoughts, including any deviations from the Four Standards, were then shared with others—often at breakfast. A person considered "off the ball" had "guidance" with others to see what should be done to get back "on the ball." The leaders of MRA seemed to have unquestioned guidance from God about almost everything and everybody. To question the guidance of the leaders was usually an indication that the doubter needed "change."

For the first few years, although I carried a black bag when traveling around the world with MRA teams, my role as a doctor was limited to dispensary work in one of the MRA centers. With the passage of time, and a dose of the reality that comes to physicians who take care of "saints" and "sinners," I wondered whether some of MRA's dicta were a little too pat, a little too general in scope. "When man listens, God speaks; when man obeys, God acts; when men change, nations change," were great headline declarations but seemed to me to lack real understanding of the forces of nature, human and otherwise, that have forged customs and cultures and even politicians over centuries. Yet, since doubters were considered sinners, often labeled as such publicly, disengagement was difficult. One's sins were used as weapons to keep a person "on the ball."

The surrender of a person's conscience and power of decision to others, no matter how good and God-guided they are—or think they are—eventually becomes a catch-22. You rely on the guidance of others to free you from sins that are then exploited by the same people to bind you to their ideas of right and wrong.

Although we sincerely believed we were engaged in something unique under God's guidance to "remake the world," the months, and later years, spent away from our children can never be recovered. They came through it, albeit with wounds that still hurt and occasionally fester. We learned a lot, painfully. Those who really sacrifice and suffer because of separations are the children. They have no say in the matter.

In 1960, during a meeting in MRA's headquarters in Caux, overlooking Montreaux and Lake Geneva, a small group was selected for a mission to the Belgian Congo six weeks before that country's independence. Included were two former Mau Mau from Kenya, a former student leader from Nigeria, a man from South Africa, and a French woman who had been a labor leader and a member of the Resistance. I was chosen to go along because I spoke French.

At the end of a meeting during which plans were made for the Congo, Tine and I walked slowly back to our room along the wide wooden hallways in the old luxury hotel. "I guess I'll take my black bag along. You never know, it might come in handy," I said.

"It might," said Tine, opening the door into our room.

We walked over to the French windows that led onto a small balcony and went out. Way below, the lake shimmered under the summer sky. "How long do you think you'll be gone?" she asked quietly.

I looked at her, but she turned away. I wanted to take her in my arms and hug her, but that was "impure" in MRA, so I stood there, an empty, hollow feeling mixing with fear of the unknown.

"They said six weeks," I replied.

We sat down on small metal chairs. She dried her eyes with a crumpled piece of Kleenex. "Well, six weeks isn't all that long."

> *Jesus said, "I tell you this: there is no one who has given up home, or wife, brothers, parents, or children, for the sake of the Kingdom of God, who will not be repaid many times over in this age, and in the age to come have eternal life."*

By following the guidance from God, checked and approved by the leaders of MRA, my future seemed bright. God, I was assured, would take care of the kids. I presumed it was right because it felt so painful. (Much later, I concluded that real hell on earth is what those closest to you experience when you are out following what you think is divine guidance.) But, at the time, uncomfortable thoughts were overshadowed by the feeling of being chosen—chosen to go into danger and the unknown for God. We were invited to sit at the head table, and what we said seemed to be slightly more important than before.

With Léopoldville, the Congolese capital, still reeling from riots, and tribal violence breaking out in the interior, it seemed clear to all that hell was about to break out in the Congo. I was fearful enough of the assignment to buy a small switchblade knife in a hardware store in Montreux. When pressed, a silver button in the handle released the blade. In retrospect it sounds silly, but I felt more secure with that small weapon in my pocket.

Looking back over a span of thirty years, I have often asked myself the question "Why did you go to Africa in 1960?" With a perspective that has grown with time and distance, I have answered, "A taste for adventure and a touch of sentimental altruism (second cousin to the effortless superiority of many colonials) fueled my journey to the Belgian Congo."

Was there a careful, rational plan that led me to the Belgian Congo? No. My antennae were tuned to opportunity and I gladly accepted challenges that came my way. The initial six weeks became sixteen years.

René Dubos defined the adventure of life for me: "Man has elected to fight, not necessarily for himself, but for a process of emotional, intellectual, and ethical growth that goes on forever. To grow in the midst of dangers is the fate of the human race, because it is the law of the spirit." I loved the fear and thrill of being chosen for a mission spiced by unknown hazards in a strange land among people with fearsome reputations. The emotions were similar to those I experienced flying combat during the war. For breakfast, fighter pilots were fed fresh eggs and bacon, transport crews ate powdered eggs. The elite accept danger, the rest are drafted as fodder for the war machines. Those chosen for sacrifice by the Mayans were treated with special esteem before their death. Life is sweeter, more filled with color and music, if death or danger lurk around the corner. But is self-sacrifice really a sacrifice of self or is it the elevation of an ego onto the altar of public recognition and esteem? Children may grow to despise parents who abandon them, especially if their parents are viewed as heroes by others.

I thought our stay in the Congo would be brief. But after starting to work in the *Hôpital des Congolais* I was completely absorbed and captivated by the work in the operating rooms. The MRA team's argument that I had abandoned my calling to change people and the world for medical work and surgery was true. I returned to my original passion very quickly. I reveled in the work and felt at home doing what I had been trained to do.

Medicine may be a demanding spouse, but surgery is a seductive mistress expert in caressing egos. One day I was driving across the main boulevard in Léopoldville, preoccupied by things other than the traffic or the cop in the middle of a busy intersection. I ignored his signal to stop. He jumped off his white and black box and ran toward my car, shaking his police stick at me, furious over my lack of respect for his authority. He bent over to look in the car, and suddenly recognizing me, a grin spread across his face. Straightening up, he tore open his shirt and pushed down his belt to expose a long scar on his belly.

"Remember, *Docteur*? You operated on me!"

"Oh, yes," I lied. We shook hands.

He stepped into the middle of the crossroads, halting all traffic so I could proceed, and saluted as I drove past.

Tine joined me in the Congo at the end of that first

year. The children remained in Switzerland at the MRA center at Caux under the care of MRA people, who in no way could replace their parents. During the early sixties Tine, for the most part, stayed with the children in the U.S. In the mid-sixties and early seventies, she commuted between her mother's home in Greenwich, Connecticut, and Africa. During some of that time, two of the children attended the American school in Kinshasa. Even then, my work at the hospital, with the president, and in my practice allowed for little time with the family. In truth, I was more comfortable dealing with professional responsibilities than with the needs at home.

Did I feel guilty about the family? Sometimes, but the weight and imperatives of my other responsibilities were effective guilt suppressors. Being a doctor meant tackling people's problems. How could I cancel medical appointments for the sick or avoid a trip with the president? Anyway, with little understanding of children or their problems, I felt useless as a father. I reasoned, or rationalized, that the children would benefit from my devotion to medical duty. And after a while that reasoning became a Pavlovian reflex to family demand. Only years later did I realize that simply being there for your own children is more important than solving their problems. It takes time and hard work to become a doctor; fatherhood, I learned so late, requires at least equal, and often more, effort and perseverance.

CHAPTER 8

Samuel

THE FIRST YEAR or so in Africa I was full of a sort of adrenaline-producing white knight mission to keep Africans from killing each other by bringing them God's guidance and the Four Standards. We were led to believe that these efforts would counter the godless tyranny of communism.

Neither I nor my teammates would have ventured into the Congo had it not been for Moral Re-Armament. We would never have dared to undertake some of our activities during the mutiny and, later, with the army, had we not felt guided and protected by God.

Three days after King Baudouin of Belgium turned the country over to the new prime minister, Patrice Lumumba, soldiers of the Congolese Army, stationed in the capital city of Léopoldville, rose up against their Belgian officers, broke into the arsenals, and went on the rampage. A massive exodus of Belgians occurred from this city of almost a million people. I, too, was eager to leave town, but couldn't: the roads to the airport had been blocked off.

Two days into the mutiny, I walked the four blocks from the MRA apartment to the *Hôpital des Congolais* to see if I could help in surgery. I hid behind trees and ran down alleys, dodging Jeeps loaded with soldiers. The hospital's front entrance was blocked by a crowd of shouting, jostling Congolese pushing against the iron grille. Policemen in gray uniforms poked their clubs through the bars, trying to push the people away. I elbowed my way to the entrance and shouted, "*Docteur. Je*

58

suis un docteur." The guards opened the gate just enough to let me through.

People with bloody rags on their heads and limbs sat passively next to a wall, waiting to be seen. Half a dozen wounded on stretchers were lined up in front of the emergency room. A Congolese in a blood-stained smock stuck his head out of the door, people shouted and waved their arms, and the nearest patient was wheeled into the building. I ran and squeezed myself in behind the stretcher and closed the door.

Four male nurses washed, debrided, and stitched the wounded in four bays furnished with simple metal operating tables and instrument stands. Everything was wet and bloody, and filthy dressings were scattered over the floor. There was little noise. The place stank of bodies and the sweetish smell of fresh blood.

"Where is the operating room?" I asked. One of the nurses looked up and pointed to a door. I went through and stepped into a four-bed room where people sat on the beds apparently recovering from their treatment. I opened another door into a long ward with beds along each wall. Congolese with legs and arms in casts, bandaged heads, and thick dressings covering chests or abdomens filled the twenty beds. Most wore parts of their olive-drab uniforms. Conversation stopped as I walked into the long ward.

"*Salle d'opération?*" I asked. One of the men pointed to the far end of the ward. "*Merci,*" I said.

"*Sale Flamand*—dirty Fleming," a man spit out as I walked past his bed. I stopped and looked at him.

"*Américain,*" I said, pointing at my chest. He glared back at me sullenly. All whites were Flamands to him.

I walked out of the far end of the ward, along a short covered walkway, and opening the screen door of a long veranda, I stepped into the surgery building. Several stretchers were lined up against the walls between two operating rooms. A nursing sister came out of the OR to the left.

"*Vous cherchez quelqu'un*—You are looking for someone?" she asked brusquely.

"*Oui, ma soeur. Je suis un chirugien Américain. Je voudrais vous aider, si possible*—I am an American surgeon. I'd like to help if possible."

"Where did you learn to speak French?"

"I was brought up in Paris."

"*Une seconde.*" She strode back into the operating room.

Looking through the screens on the veranda, I could see the outside of the pavilion I had walked through. Off to the right other low yellow brick pavilions surrounded by covered terraces were connected to a large central walkway by smaller concrete paths. The grass between the buildings was freshly cut and uncluttered. I could hear the clamor of people around the emergency room.

"*Docteur?*" I turned and saw a small thin man in a surgical gown and hat, his mask pulled down to his neck. Behind him was a Congolese similarly dressed. He peeled off his right glove, and we shook hands.

"Pirquin," he said.

"Close," I replied. "Can I give you a hand?"

"Can you take X rays?"

"No. But I'm sure I can learn if you show me."

"Come with me." He pulled off his other glove and his bloody gown and tossed them to the Congolese. He led the way through the screen door onto the walkway and into the trauma ward. The wounded followed us with their eyes. Pirquin opened the door into a small room off the ward that housed an old X-ray machine.

"Here's a chart which gives you the settings for various X rays. If the picture is too dark give it more volts. If the contrast is not clear enough give it more amps. But try and get it right the first time, we may have a hard time getting film if this chaos continues." He showed me how to develop and fix the film in the baths.

"The patients on stretchers outside the operating rooms have fractures or wounds of their extremities. X-ray them and bring me the results. Should be easy enough for you, even the Congolese can do it."

We walked back through the silent, threatening patients. Pirquin strode ahead with his chin out. The ward could have been empty for all the recognition he gave the men in bed. Hate and bitterness were palpable and explosive. I was embarrassed and very frightened. I felt like an intruder in a family fight. I'd never been in such an atmosphere before. Back in surgery, the sister was waiting.

Pirquin introduced me. "This is Dr. Close. He'll take X rays."

"Good. Your next patient is ready," replied the sister.

"Thank you. See you later, Close," said the old surgeon as he walked into the OR.

I turned to the sister. "What is your name?"

"I am La Mère Germaine, in charge of the operating rooms." She turned and, as if calling a dog to heel, shouted, "Samuel, Samuel, *ici!*"

A man came out of one of the rooms to the right and approached slowly.

"Samuel is my assistant," announced the sister. "Samuel, this is Dr. Close, an American. He will X-ray the patients that need it."

I stuck out my hand, but he didn't take it.

"*Américain?*" he asked with a sneer.

"Yes."

"I listen to Radio Moscow every morning."

"Oh," I said, surprised. "Well, maybe you can help me wheel these patients to the X-ray room." He pulled a stretcher to the door and pushed it out. I followed.

During the morning Samuel and I worked together. He stood by with a long-suffering look on his face as I carefully adjusted and checked the controls on the X-ray machine.

"Do you know how to do this?" I asked him.

"Of course."

"Then why don't you do it? We could go faster."

"It is not my job."

"What is your job?"

"I am the operating-room chief."

"I thought—"

"That was three days ago, before Independence. The new hospital director will come tomorrow to order the sister to give me the keys to the instrument and medicine cabinets," said Samuel. "The Belgians are finished here."

"Is a Congolese surgeon going to replace Dr. Pirquin?" I asked.

"We have no Congolese surgeons. None have been trained."

After taking the X rays, I helped Pirquin reduce and cast the fractures that hadn't needed surgery. Some patients required small doses of IV pentothal, which was administered by Samuel. We worked in silence. Only the sister barked out orders to the Congolese "boys." Pirquin worked rapidly and skillfully. His thin face, deeply furrowed on either side of an aquiline nose and small mouth, was fixed in a tired, tight-lipped expression. Under bushy gray eyebrows, his eyes were hard behind frameless bifocals, but he molded and smoothed plaster over broken limbs with care and artistry.

"Hold the foot carefully while the plaster hardens, and don't dig in with your fingers; it will make pressure points."

I felt like telling him I was good with plaster, but didn't. As I sat there waiting for the plaster to harden, I watched the others going about their duties.

Felix, Eugene, and old Tata Pierre made up the rest of the operating-room crew. Each of them came up to me and introduced himself, offering a hand with quiet dignity. We shook hands and they smiled. Felix and Eugene assisted in the OR, and Tata Pierre worked the old steam sterilizer that hissed and gurgled in a corner of the instrument room. A diminutive Congolese with a short forehead and deep-set eyes named Makila pushed a large soggy mop around the OR. He glanced at me as he mopped the plaster off the tiled floor around the stretchers.

From time to time another patient on a gurney was wheeled in and put at the end of the line on the veranda. Sister Germaine greeted each newcomer with, "Not another! When will it finish?" Grabbing the stretcher and waving the ward "boy" out of the door, she examined the patient and attended to what preliminary washing, dressing, and splinting were needed. She worked efficiently with her hands, but her tongue lashed out if the patient moved or complained.

"*Ninganga te, zoba*—Don't move, idiot!"

Although most of the patients were silent, some moaned softly. They seemed resigned to whatever fate or the sister had in store for them.

The sister was a small woman, somewhere in her late thirties or early forties. It was difficult to judge age in a nun. The long skirt of her uniform, cut above the ankle, swayed as she moved. She tied her white apron snugly around her waist, giving her bust some prominence. A tight wimple framed her face and chin, and a starched headpiece, which rose up from the wimple, carried a broad veil over the top of her head and down to the back of her shoulders. Her green eyes had no smile lines at the corners. Her nostrils flared when she gave an order. Small wisps of blond hair escaped from the cloth at her temples, and her lower lip was full and petulant. Samuel moved sullenly and made no effort to hide his hatred for this woman. Felix and the others obeyed promptly, apparently used to her gruff tone.

The shouting around the emergency room had died down. Pirquin and I were wrapping plaster around the leg of a man with a fractured tibia. Felix handed us rolls of plaster he had dipped in a bucket of water. In the distance we heard a siren approaching the hospital. I looked at Pirquin; he shrugged his shoulders. All of a sudden there was an explosion on the tin roof over our heads, followed by a series of lesser blasts. We dove to the floor. A large green coconut rolled off the roof and landed next to the palm tree that stood at the entrance of the building. Felix laughed as Pirquin and I got up.

The sister yelled, "*Tika*—Enough Felix."

We finished the cast and were washing the plaster off our hands when two ward "boys" came running down the walkway pushing a gurney. A Congolese soldier, clutching a bloody towel covering his belly, was screaming in pain. As he was wheeled into the veranda loops of intestine slithered out from between his fingers.

In an instant the soldier was carried to the operating table. The sister replaced the towel with a large abdominal pad, which Felix held firmly in place. Samuel strapped the patient's arm to a board and started an IV. Pirquin walked over to the sink and started to scrub. He motioned to me with his head to follow suit, and ordered Samuel to induce the patient with pentothal, then use gas, oxygen, and ether.

The man had been slashed across the abdomen with a machete, opening up a gash of six inches into his peritoneal cavity. The sister swabbed iodine and alcohol onto the abdominal wall, then she and I placed a large drape with a hole in the center over the patient as Felix let go of the pad and stepped away from the table. The soldier coughed as Samuel added ether to the gas and oxygen. His intestines writhed out over the drape; Pirquin and I quickly covered them with large, wet abdominal pads. He clamped some bleeders in the omentum and I tied them off. Then the old surgeon carefully examined every inch of bowel. It had escaped injury. With me pulling on the sides of the wound, Pirquin pushed the intestines back into the abdomen. We washed out the peritoneal cavity with saline, dumped some penicillin and streptomycin powder into the wound, and closed with through-and-through sutures of heavy stainless steel, leaving a soft rubber drain sticking out from the side. The operation had taken less than forty minutes. Throughout that time, in spite of the tension and fear that gripped all of us, Pirquin never lost his concentration or thoroughness. We walked out to the veranda to set the fractures still waiting to be reduced.

It was eight P.M. by the time we finished work. Pirquin gave me a ride back to the apartment.

"You'll be there in the morning?" he asked.

"Yes, if you want me to be."

"I do," he said. We shook hands and he drove off. I returned to the MRA apartment and, after a cold dinner, went to bed, too tired to go into details of the day with the others.

When I walked in the next morning at eight, Pirquin was already at work on a Belgian whose head and shoulders were drenched in blood from a huge scalp wound. The man's wife was sitting in a corner of the OR with her arm in a splint. She was crying softly, with her face buried in Sister Germaine's apron.

I stood in the doorway and heard the woman sob, "It was our own houseboy. And after all we have done for him."

"What do you expect?" snapped the sister bitterly. "They're all animals, *macaques*—monkeys out of the trees." She was oblivious of Eugene, who was helping Pirquin. She looked up, saw me, and said, "There are some blacks you can look at on the veranda. I told Samuel to help you in the other operating room."

Three patients were lined up on gurneys next to the screen door. One was holding his swollen jaw in his hands. I opened my mouth and made a biting motion. He tried to do the same thing slowly, but winced with pain. His upper and lower teeth were way out of line. I'd never fixed a broken jaw. I'd have to wait for Pirquin. The next patient had a soggy dressing over his face and mouth. I pulled his hand away gently and saw a jagged laceration of his cheek and lips. His eye was swollen shut and purple. The third patient's hands clutched at a huge incarcerated hernia in his groin. He lay in his vomit. Samuel was at my side.

"We'd better do this one first," I said, pulling the hernia patient's stretcher toward the operating room next to where Pirquin was working.

"I'll give him a spinal," said Samuel.

"Fine. I'll change my clothes and be right back."

The operation went well. Samuel was an able assistant. The hernia contained a loop of gangrenous small bowel that had been forced into the sac and had died when its blood supply had been squeezed off. I resected the dead bowel, sewed the healthy ends together, and repaired the hernia. I thanked God for my Roosevelt Hospital training.

As we were closing, three more white people were brought into Pirquin's room. From what I could hear, they had been mauled by an angry mob near the parliament building. A moment later a stretcher was pushed into my room with a huge Congolese soldier crying out with pain from a wound that had opened up his right thigh. The stretcher was soaked with blood. Three other soldiers in full combat gear, waving FAL automatic weapons, accompanied the wounded man.

"Shot by a Belgian paratrooper," growled one of the soldiers.

Samuel and one of the soldiers lifted the hernia patient off the table, put him on a stretcher, and parked him on the veranda. The soldiers heaved the wounded man onto the table. Samuel slit the tunic sleeve, pushed in a needle, and started an IV. I injected pentothal into the tubing. The patient relaxed and slept. Samuel put an airway in his mouth and kept him down with oxygen and a little nitrous oxide.

The bullet had penetrated the inner part of his thigh about halfway down to the knee. The wound of exit was a gaping hole the size of my fist on the lateral aspect of his thigh. Dark venous blood oozed from shredded muscle and streams of bright red blood spurted from arteries. I stuffed gauze pads into the wound and pulled over the same basin of soapy water I had used to rinse my gloves off during the previous operation. After washing off the skin next to the wound, I draped sterile towels around the wound and went to work. I clamped and tied the bleeders and explored the wound with my hand. Several bone spicules had been blasted off the femur, but the bone itself was not fractured all the way across the shaft. I tied off more bleeders, pulled out as many of the bone fragments as I could feel, cut out dead muscle, and sewed together what was left to reestablish the normal anatomy of the muscle groups as much as possible.

We had run out of plain and chromic catgut. I asked Samuel if he'd go next door and get some from Pirquin's room, but he refused—mumbling invectives about the sister and whites as a whole. I left the table and headed for the door to the veranda. Two soldiers blocked my way. "You can't leave. If you don't save our man I'll kill you," said the bigger man.

Samuel told them I needed to get more sutures to close the wound. They let me pass into the next room. The sister gave me the sutures.

Pirquin asked, "Do you have an extra tank of nitrous in your room?"

"I think so."

"Could you bring it in? The sister doesn't want to go next door," he said.

"That's ridiculous," I snapped. "For God's sake why not?"

The sister replied tightly, "*Ils me font peur*—They scare me."

"They're scared of you," I said. "I'll bring the tank in when I'm through."

I went back to my patient. Sam was pressing a pad in the wound to stop the oozing from torn muscles. The soldiers glowered, their helmets almost hiding their eyes and their guns at the ready with fingers on triggers.

"Samuel, tell them to get out."

"It won't do any good. They'll go when you're through with their brother."

After cutting away the skin adjacent to the wound of entry, I ran several large soft rubber drains across the whole thigh to drain both sides. "Samuel, I was thinking about you this morning," I said as I placed sutures in the wound margins.

"You were? What were you thinking?" he said, without looking up.

"I was thinking," I said slowly, "that it's probably the attitude of superiority and arrogance in us whites that has made you bitter. I'm sorry about that, but some of us are trying to put that right."

He stared at me for a long moment, then said, "That is the first time I ever heard a white man admit he could be wrong."

After we had wheeled the soldier into the trauma ward, we took care of the patients on the veranda. Pirquin showed me how to use an external appliance to secure the fragments of the man's broken jaw. More casualties came in. Some we lost: like the man whose head was all but severed from his neck by a machete. Some died from simple blood loss—the blood bank was empty.

Night had fallen and the curfew brought an eerie calm broken only by the howl of abandoned dogs. Pirquin showered, and the sister and the "boys" cleaned up and prepared sterile packs of instruments and drapes for the morning. I stepped outside and sat on a bench by the door. A gentle night breeze rattled the fronds of the palm tree and cooled the sweat in my OR greens. I thought of all the Saturday nights in the emergency room at the Roosevelt. The blood here was the same color; the pain and fear no different. The violence in New York sprang from turf wars among Puerto Rican and white gangs, like in *West Side Story*. Here the violence was also racial and tribal. But the hatred and bitterness we had lived through today seemed more glandular, more emotional and less calculated than at home. Maybe our "civilization" was only a thin veneer of police control partially isolating us from the savage part of human nature.

The screen door opened behind me and slammed shut. Samuel approached and knelt down in front of me. He started to wipe the blood and plaster off my shoes.

"Sam, you don't need to do that," I said, pulling away my feet, embarrassed by his attention. He stood up and walked back into the OR. I followed him, but he was out the back door before I could catch up. Pirquin came out of the dressing room. "*A demain*—See you tomorrow," he said.

"*A demain*," I replied.

I showered, and by the time I was through, everyone had left. I let myself out of the hospital through the small back door behind the OR which the nuns used. I walked briskly down the street, staying in the shadow of the wall that surrounded the hospital. As I came to the avenue where our apartment house stood, I heard a car racing toward me. I tucked myself behind a large flame tree. A Jeep roared past. I ran the rest of the way, bounded up the stairs, and pounded on the door of our apartment. One of the MRA team let me in.

"Where have you been? We've been worried about you."

"At the hospital. I'll tell you about it later." I went to my room and, too tired to eat, was asleep as soon as I hit the mattress.

Over the next couple of weeks our workload increased as other surgical services in the city ceased functioning because of clashes among the personnel. As Samuel and I operated on patients together we talked about our families and about human nature and the trouble it sometimes generated when our judgments were clouded by hate and pride. Sam brought his wife and small son, Hi-Fi, to meet me. I introduced Sam and his family to some of my MRA friends. But in spite of the fact that Samuel and I were working well together, the hostility between him and *la Mère* Germaine continued. She snapped orders at him, which he either pretended not to hear or obeyed sullenly. Pirquin had retreated into a shell of gloom and silence. Then one morning, as I was talking to the sister about the day's schedule, Sam joined us.

"What is it, Samuel?" I asked.

He turned to the sister. "Over the past few days I have thought a lot. I have hated you and other Belgians for the way you have treated me and my people. I know we cannot go on this way, and I would like to ask your forgiveness for my bitterness. I need your help to be different."

The sister stared at him wide-eyed and her face went as white as her veil. She turned away and walked out of the operating room. She stayed away all day. The next morning she didn't show up. I walked across the street to the convent and asked to see the mother superior. She came out of her office and greeted me.

"I came to find out if Sister Germaine is all right. We need her very much in the operating room," I said.

"The sister spent most of the night in the chapel on her knees," said the mother superior quietly. "I don't think you need to worry, she will come over a little later." I thanked her and returned to work.

In midafternoon the sister walked into the operating pavilion and called Samuel. He came out of the instrument room. I was on the veranda casting a fracture.

"Samuel, I am the one who needs forgiveness," she said, her voice barely audible. "I have bitterly resented the way your people have treated us after all we have done for you. I've been terrified of being beaten or raped like some of the other white women. I have betrayed my vows. I am the one who needs forgiveness and your help."

Sam was stunned. He walked out of the pavilion but returned in a little while. The three of us sat down and talked about how to best manage our growing workload.

CHAPTER 9

The Old Surgeon and His Horse

DURING MOST of that first year there were only three doctors for the whole hospital: I was in surgery and Paul Beheyt, a Belgian internist, covered medicine for the fifteen hundred beds. An Egyptian called Bill Morgan did OB-GYN. He and the midwives averaged 120 deliveries a day. Sister Germaine became my nurse and assistant. We had no lab, and I did my own gas-oxygen-ether anesthesia. I taught Makila, our small, monosyllabic floor sweeper, to hold the mask on the patient's face and push on the balloon in rhythm with his own breathing. Makila means "blood" in Lingala. Pierre said he was part pygmy. Makila was calm and unflappable, and proud of his new responsibilities. Over the next year we averaged 350 operations a month.

One evening in August of 1960, several weeks after the troops were back in their barracks and calm returned to the streets of the capital, Dr. Pirquin invited me to Léopoldville's *cercle hippique* for an evening ride on the club's Thoroughbreds. The club was in Binza, a residential suburb on a hill overlooking the city and the river.

We started at five, trotting up and down hills through tall grasses leading to the river. At first the mosquitoes weren't bad, but after crossing a stream that emptied into a marsh, they became fierce. Half an hour later we crested high ground and looked out over the Congo River. To our right the rapids started below the Stanley Pool. Across the water on the Brazzaville side, flattened tops of giant trees

72

were silhouetted against a red-and-yellow sky. A breeze softened the pounding heat of the day. Parrots, chattering and squawking, flew northward in their disorganized way, flapping toward their night perches upriver on M'Bamu Island. High above, hundreds of fruit bats sailed slowly south. The horses played with their bits and pawed the ground, impatient to get back to their stables and grain. We held them still and watched a full moon emerge from the forest on the distant bank. Below us, the river split around Monkey Island, hurling itself against massive boulders. Colors faded into shades of gray, and boiling spume turned to shimmering silver.

Carefully, I followed Pirquin down a steep incline into a palm grove bathed in moonlight. Some of the trees had been trimmed; in others, palm nuts in clusters the size of beer kegs hung below the fronds. Short grasses carpeted the ground between the rows of trees. I caught up with him, and we rode into the grove side by side.

I turned to him and remarked, "This is a peaceful place."

The old surgeon looked straight ahead, sitting his Arabian stallion like a riding master. "Last night two men were killed in the village we're coming to. The natives have destroyed the tranquillity since Independence. They will ruin all we have done in this country," he growled. We rode on a little. "The liberals in Brussels are just as guilty," he added. "Some of us have spent a lifetime forging the best medical system in Africa. We brought discipline and order to the Congo. Rabble-rousers like Lumumba were put in prison, and the natives were made to work. They're a lazy bunch, you know."

"I don't know," I said. "This is my first time in Africa."

"You Americans are *des enfants naïfs*. You have ideals but many illusions." He gave a short humorless laugh. "You think if everyone is free to do as they please, the world will turn rose-colored."

I resisted the temptation to argue. "I'm sure we have much to learn."

Pirquin reined in his horse, and I followed suit; we faced each other. Moonlight glanced off his glasses, and his mouth was a thin line under a hawkish nose. A night bird called, and tree frogs croaked like wooden rattles. He continued with clipped intensity.

"Brussels precipitated Independence. The Congo was costing too much, and the bureaucrats panicked when riots erupted last year. We *colons* knew the natives weren't ready to govern themselves."

"And no one listened to you?" I asked.

"Of course not. We told them it would take another ten years, at least, to train the Congolese adequately." He leaned forward in the saddle. "Listen, *confrère*. We've taught most of them to read, but there's still only a handful of university graduates. Now that they are on their own again, they'll hack each other to pieces as they did before we colonized them. *Nom de Dieu*, just look at the massacres going on right now between the Balubas and the Luluas." He stopped, uncomfortable perhaps with so many words. "We'd better keep going," he said, spurring his horse into a trot. I followed, and after a little while he slowed to a walk.

He waved toward a small fishing village just visible in the moonlight. "There's where the bodies were found by the police this morning."

"Why were the men killed?" I asked, feeling my gut tighten.

"Who knows? Family problems, a drunken fight over a woman, an old vendetta—you can't tell with them. The point is that before independence fear of the authorities tamed their bestiality."

The village curved around a sandy cove off the main

channel of the river, whose roar now drowned out the noises of the night. Pirogues were drawn up on the beach with throwing nets resting in their shallow bows. A dozen mud and wattle houses thatched with palm fronds squatted under broad-leafed trees. Thin gray ribbons of smoke rose from cooking fires to be lost in the dark foliage of mango trees. The smell of rotting vegetation and firewood filled the air, and people, squatting or sitting on low stools around fires, were dimly lit by the flames.

Children ran toward us, jumping up and down, yelling "*Punda*—horse, *punda, punda*." Several of the older ones came to pat our mounts as we stopped.

"*Mbote,*" we said to the fishermen.

"*Mbote, mundele*—Hello, white man," they answered dully. A driftwood log cracked under a cooking pot and shot sparks into a column of smoke. I saw the glint of a machete as a man stood up, stared, then was lost in shadow. The brooding hostility was only partly relieved by the innocent delight of the youngsters.

"*Keba, mwana*—Watch out, children," Pirquin ordered. They scampered away, and we rode past the huts and the silent people. Leaving the village behind was a relief. Pirquin sat ramrod stiff with his chin out, walking his stallion slowly and deliberately. We climbed a small hill, and the horses broke into a trot as the lights of the riding club came into view.

We dismounted at the clubhouse. Congolese grooms led our horses away. Pirquin and I walked up the steps and into the bar. He was greeted with handshakes and a quiet, "*Docteur.*" He introduced me to his friends as *mon confrère Américain*. The gray-haired barman filled two mugs from a frosty bottle of Primus. Pirquin nodded his thanks. We clicked glasses and drank.

"I heard you were leaving," said one of the men nearby.

"Yes, I'm flying out tomorrow with Van der Pic, the police *commissaire*. He was seriously wounded in last night's clash with the army," replied the old surgeon.

"Will you be able to get a little rest? How long will you be away?"

"Who knows?" Pirquin looked into his beer mug then turned away and walked out onto the porch. I followed.

"I wouldn't go if it weren't for the *commissaire*," he said bitterly.

"I am sure of that. You belong here."

He glanced at me, took a long drink, then sat on the step. I joined him.

After a moment he said, "I'm glad you came to the hospital to help me. I hate to leave you alone on the service, but the sister knows what to do."

"And Samuel," I added.

"And Samuel," he repeated. "But you'll have to watch him. He has Arab blood. He's smart like a fox."

The man who had spoken to Pirquin walked out from the bar and put another bottle of beer on the step between us. "*Bon voyage, Docteur,*" he said, and left.

Pirquin carefully poured beer down the side of my mug and handed it to me. He filled his with equal care and, turning to me, raised it—"*Chin*"—without a smile.

"*Chin,*" I replied.

The cold beer tasted good. Laughter came from inside the clubhouse, but the old man's somber mood cast a pall over the night.

Shafts of yellow light came from the box stalls off to our left. The sound of hooves stamping and the chattering of men's voices floated up the steps as the grooms hosed down one of the horses. In the clubhouse, people were saying *bonne nuit* and heading for their cars. We sat together in silence, Pirquin staring ahead, occasionally drinking his beer. Behind us all was quiet except for the clinking of glasses as the bartender tidied up. A single bulb glowed over the door to the bar. In the distance, where dark sky met horizon, a band of gray lay over the center of the city.

I glanced at the old surgeon; it was painful to see him so depressed. I thought of our conversation a few days ago as we were sewing up the thigh of a soldier whose femur had been shattered by a bullet. Pirquin had sketched, in a flat monotone, his thirty years in the Congo, starting with earlier duties in the interior working in small hospitals, on call all the time. His wife had died of cerebral malaria. His son, a doctor, returned to Belgium and an easier, more lucrative practice. Eventually Pirquin was assigned to the capital: surgery and his horse became his life. I asked the sister how he lost the ring finger on his right hand. She told me the Congolese liked to say that a patient chewed it off, but Pirquin told her it had been amputated years ago because of an infection. In the operating room he inverted the fourth finger of a rubber glove into his palm and worked with skill and speed.

Pirquin emptied his mug and turned to me. In the dim light his eyes looked infinitely weary and sad. He waved toward the stable where his stallion, Lynx, was being rubbed down.

"It's like a knife in my belly to think I may never see my horse again."

"I understand," I said softly. I thought of Tine's old gelding, Skookum. "My wife had a chestnut hunter back in Connecticut in the days when we fell in love and spent our evenings riding in the moonlight. Then I was sent to Texas for pilot training, and Tine sold Skookum so she could come with me. After the war we returned to the East Coast and tried to find him. He'd apparently become a parade horse, but after that, all we could find out was that he was sold several times. Someone told us he might be in upstate New York—his trail had vanished.

"One day we were driving into Greenwich on a back road, and Tine yelled, 'Stop! There's Skookum!' She jumped out of the car, climbed through the fence, and ran toward an old horse in the middle of a field. His lower lip hung down, and his head seemed too heavy for his neck. As she approached, his ears came forward, one at a time. Tine stopped in front of him and cried out, 'Shake hands, Skook.' His head came up, and he lifted his right front leg. She hugged him and kissed his soft nose and scratched him behind his ears. We bought him back on the spot, and he lived with us for the rest of his life."

Pirquin stood and motioned me to follow him. We walked down the steps to the stable. Lynx was almost dry after his bath, his halter rope looped over the hitching rail in front of his stall.

"*Un moment,*" he said to the groom, who stopped his work, moved to the horse's head, and held him steady on a long lead. The stallion looked down at the doctor, his ears forward, nostrils dilating in expectation.

"*Salut,* Lynx," commanded Pirquin. The horse lifted his right foreleg and held it up until the doctor touched the hoof. He laid his hand on the animal's proud neck, then spun around and walked back to the clubhouse. Once again we sat on the steps. After a while the old surgeon turned to me, his tears bright in the starlight. "You must ride him after I go," he whispered.

I nodded. "But you'll be back. This is your life. The people need you here."

We looked up as his horse was led to the foot of the steps. The groom whispered a command, and the stallion reared up and pawed the night air in a farewell salute. Then the groom bowed and led the horse away.

Pirquin stood and quickly turned toward the parking

lot. I followed him to his car. He got in, started the engine, and looked up at me.

"It was my life, but it is finished. Good night, Close. *Adieu*."

He drove away rapidly.

CHAPTER 10

Soeur Marie Euphrasie and the Night Mère

THE SURGICAL DIVISION for which I was responsible consisted of two hundred beds divided into three pavilions. Pavilion 6, or P6, was divided into two wards, old men on one side, children on the other. I was the only surgeon.

La Soeur Marie Euphrasie was in charge of P6. She was somewhere in her late fifties and large. She had high blood pressure. Her ankles were swollen most of the time, and she walked with a side-to-side gait because of stiff hips. Innumerable minute smile lines framed her mouth and eyes.

A few of the old men in the ward had terminal cancer. Most of the other patients were recovering from prostate surgery. I did suprapubic prostatectomies, taking huge prostates out from within the bladder. Before closing the wounds, I threaded a large catheter up into the bladder and snugged the water-filled balloon on the catheter into the prostatic bed. Once the patient was in his bed on the ward, traction was provided by a string tied to the catheter and stretched over the foot of the bed to a small weight. The system worked well, provided the whole patient wasn't pulled to the end of the bed by the weight. This was the sister's invention. We had no blood bank, so postoperative bleeding was something we tried to avoid at all cost.

A small two-bed room was part of P6. The sister used these beds for dying patients, or patients with tetanus or rabies. She had a high batting average for the tetanus patients. The rabies patients, however, died rather horribly.

The other ward in P6 housed postoperative children. Many of them were recovering from injuries caused by the fighting in the city. Tina, my oldest daughter, had sent me a supply of bubble gum for the kids, and one morning between operations I showed them how to blow rubber bubbles. Then I handed out two sticks to each kid and told them to see who could blow the biggest bubble. I went back to the operating room. About a half hour later, while I was operating on a man with a twisted colon, *la Soeur* Marie Euphrasie stormed into the operating room and roundly chewed me out. She was furious because the children's faces, hands, and sheets were covered with *caoutchouc*—rubber. I told her I would come and help her clean up the mess.

"Never mind," she said, storming out. "You've helped enough already!"

I went to P6 after I finished the operation. She had everything back to normal. The kids were all sitting at attention in their beds, trying to look serious. The sister was still rumbling away as she tended her charges.

One morning the mother of the night (we called her the night *mère*), a thin ascetic nun and a very competent nurse, was waiting for me when I arrived at the hospital.

"*Bonjour, ma mère,*" I said. "I hope you had a good night."

"Please come with me, Doctor," she replied, all business and tight lips.

I followed her into P1, our trauma ward off the emergency room. She stopped at a bed in the middle of the ward. There, lying under a sheet, either sleeping or unconscious, was a huge Ghanaian soldier with bandages covering his head and arms. Two Ghanaian MPs, a sergeant and a private wearing the blue berets and insignia of the United Nations, were at the bedside. When I came up they came to attention. "Suh," said the sergeant as he saluted.

"*Voilà!*" said the night *mère*, pointing with a straight arm and accusing index finger to the unconscious man in the bed. "This man, this soldier, came in drunk last night. He ran his truck into a tree and was brought into the emergency room. We sewed up his head and arms and put him in bed. In the middle of the night, he got out of bed and ran, completely naked, down the hall and climbed over the wall into the maternity division. He frightened all the little mothers. I called the military police. Please get rid of him."

"Thank you, *ma mère*," I said. "I'll take care of it. You get some rest." Off she went.

The two Ghanaian MPs were still at attention. They watched the night *mère* leave the ward with obvious relief.

"Relax," I said to them. They relaxed and gave me big grins. "Thank you for coming. I guess you'll get him out of here when he's awake. Right?"

"Yes, suh. Thank you, suh," snapped the sergeant.

"How are you men getting on with the people here?" I asked them out of curiosity.

"Bloody savages, suh. Don't speak Queen's English, suh," said the sergeant.

"Well . . . thank you for your help."

They snapped to attention, said "Suh," and saluted.

One night, after a long stretch of operating, I crawled into the sack late. The phone rang. It was two in the morning. It was the night *mère*.

"There is an elephant in the maternity," she announced with clipped precision.

"Come on, Mother, it's two in the morning," I said, as I would to any normal nurse.

"I do not joke," she said severely, "especially in the middle of the night. Will you please come; our little mothers are very frightened."

I felt like saying, Call the OB doctor, dammit, that's his division. This little doctor is exhausted. But I didn't. I went.

Sure enough, a baby elephant, attracted by the smell of fresh bread destined for the "little mothers' " breakfast, had pushed open the gate between the hospital and the zoo and was popping rolls into his mouth as fast as his trunk could move. We had no trouble chasing him back to the zoo.

CHAPTER 11

Gorilla Hormones

I WAS ON A SHEEP FARM in South Africa's Karoo for a two-week vacation when a call came from the U.S. Embassy in Pretoria. The president wanted me back in the Congo to take over the army medical corps and to run an errand for the United Nations. The day after I returned, Mr. Robert Gardiner, the Ghanaian head of the United Nations in the Congo, called me to say that the Russians were worried about Mr. Muzinga's welfare on the prison island of Mbula Mbemba. They had apparently suggested that Western powers were trying to kill him.

Following the assassination of Patrice Lumumba, the Congo's first prime minister, Antoine Muzinga had inherited his political and ideological cloak. He had tried to set up a separatist government in Stanleyville in the northeast corner of the country. Troops loyal to the central government had arrested him in spite of his personal bodyguard of amazonian women in military uniforms. He had been judged a traitor and exiled to Mbula Mbemba.

Mr. Gardiner was an African economist of distinction. His soft-spoken impeccable English and his calm demeanor brought a certain quiet diplomacy into the Congo United Nations Mission. He asked me to fly down to the island at the mouth of the Congo River to check things out again. He added that Mr. Muzinga's personal physician, Dr. Husseini, wanted to go along to see his patient, and would I mind taking him with me.

Early next morning, I drove to the small Ndolo airfield near the center of the city. The inevitable collection of bored soldiers lounged around the entry gate. The waiting room was empty except for a dapper little man dressed in a black suit and one of those gray-patterned silk ties worn with cutaways at weddings and diplomatic functions. He sat on a bench with a patent-leather briefcase on his lap and stood as I approached. He bowed slightly as we shook hands and handed me a card introducing himself as Dr. Hussein Husseini. Under his name was printed DOCTOR OF PSYCHOLOGY, SEXOLOGY, AND ENDOCRINOLOGY. His address was somewhere in Yemen. He opened his briefcase and pulled out an eight-by-ten glossy black-and-white photograph of himself taking blood out of the arm of a gorilla.

"My real specialty is the use of gorilla hormone in humans," he announced with quiet authority and obvious pride.

I was impressed . . . and a little nervous.

Dr. Husseini and I climbed aboard a 1936 de Havilland *Dragon Rapide* and headed for the coast. The aircraft was a biplane with two tiny engines sitting on each of the lower wings, which, along with the fuselage, were covered with patched fabric. The pilot sat up in the pointed nose while the passengers wedged into narrow canvas seats. The plane belonged to Air Brousse—Bush Air. The trip was a roller-coaster ride. We wove in and out of towering cumulus clouds over gorges of the Congo River and jagged ridges of the Crystal Mountains, which separated the capital city from the coast.

We landed on the airstrip next to Moanda, a resort village along the small strip of beach that marked the western limit of the country. After lunch at the Mangrove Hotel, we were driven to a wooden pier, where we boarded an old pilot launch and chugged out to the island in the middle of the delta.

Mbula Mbemba means "kill the mosquito." The island was a coastal artillery fortress during the Second World

War. Huge guns in concrete emplacements, a small-gauge railway, and run-down troop quarters remained. The guns and the rails had rusted and in many places were hidden by thick vines and bush. Ancient baobabs with large wooden pods hanging from limbs that seemed too thin for the giant trunks were draped with hanging moss, giving the island a creepy, mysterious undertone. Part of the shore was mangrove swamp. The croaking of frogs and the whine of a million mosquitoes filled the silence of this sinister place. As we approached the concrete dock I thought of those Charles Addams cartoons in *The New Yorker*. I half expected to see a gaunt woman dressed in flowing rags appear from the choking vegetation leading by a chain a toad-eyed little monster of a child drooling between its fangs. The caption would have been, Did you bring the ice cream?

We were met by the prison commander, *le Capitaine* Welo. I had treated him for a recurrent infection in the past, and we were on the best of terms. He was built like a sumo wrestler. I introduced him to my medical colleague, and we walked along the railway to the central building, which had been the officers' club and was now a prison.

Mr. Muzinga was delighted to see his doctor, and after they embraced each other, we were led to his room. Muzinga wore a red brocade bathrobe on the back of which was an ornate, fierce-looking dragon—a gift from the Chinese during his reign in Stanleyville. He had grown a beard and put on a few pounds since my last visit. He looked well and seemed quite relaxed. After apologizing for the spartan furnishings of the room, he invited us to sit, then engaged Dr. Husseini in a rapid exchange in Swahili, which I didn't understand.

Suddenly Husseini turned to me. "Mr. Muzinga needs some medicine to make him feel better. I will inject him with a dose of gorilla hormone." He opened his briefcase and took out a syringe and a small vial. Alarm bells jangled in my head.

I leaned forward and tried to see what was written on the vial. "Look, *confrère*," I said. "I am responsible to the authorities for Mr. Muzinga's good health. I have no experience with gorilla hormone. I cannot let you give him that shot."

The doctor from Yemen looked stunned. "What? Are you trying to prevent me from treating my patient?" I nodded. He stood abruptly and shouted, "You do not respect my opinion. I am a professor and an expert in gorilla hormones. I know what I am doing. Mr. Muzinga needs this now."

I thought that for all I knew, gorilla hormone might be great . . . or it could be poison. What were the side effects of gorilla hormone? Was it male or female? Was the stuff sterile? The indications for gorilla hormone were a mystery to me. Fleeting headlines in scandal sheets flashed through my mind: MONKEY GLAND TRANSPLANT MAKES OLD MAN POTENT . . . IMPLANTED GOAT TESTICLES PRODUCE BEARD ON HAIRLESS JANITOR. My resolve stiffened.

"I do not think Mr. Muzinga needs the injection," I stated firmly.

"This is an insult! You know nothing about these things!" shouted the Yemeni, waving the syringe and vial in front of my face.

"I admit to that."

"Then you have no right to interfere," he declared triumphantly.

In desperation I turned to Muzinga, who sat watching our exchange with a smile. I said, "Let's leave the decision to Mr. Muzinga," and proceeded to make my case.

"Mr. Muzinga, I have taken good care of you since you have been on this island, and I think you have trusted me.

It is my opinion that you do not need gorilla hormone, and I do not want you to take this injection."

To my relief he laughed. "I agree. I don't need any gorilla hormone today."

Husseini, now livid with rage, shouted, "All right, then, I will give him his insulin."

"Insulin!" I exclaimed. "Why do you want to give him insulin? He's not a diabetic."

"He needs it for his appetite!"

"There's nothing wrong with his appetite," I shouted back. "He's gained weight since the last time I was here." Here I was on more secure ground.

"He needs insulin," countered the Yemeni, diving into his briefcase again.

"You will not give him anything," I commanded. "Mr. Muzinga is not a diabetic. Anyway, his food will not be here for several hours, and I assume you know as well as I do that if you give him insulin without food you could kill him." I shouted for Welo, who came running with two MPs. "Captain, please remove this man from the building. He is endangering the life of your prisoner."

The captain gave the order, and the two MPs took Husseini by the elbows and led him out, still screaming about my lack of knowledge.

Muzinga and I spent a few more minutes together. He thanked me for the visit, and I left.

Welo and I walked back to the pilot boat. He asked me if I would call on his wife and kids in the capital and see that they were all well. He hoped to get leave in a couple of months. We shook hands and I climbed on board.

As we chugged back to the coast the Yemeni doctor was all smiles. "You thought I was trying to kill Mr. Muzinga, didn't you?" I did not reply.

We flew upriver to the capital. I stepped into the cockpit and requested the pilot to radio the airport and arrange for security police to meet the plane. As soon as we landed I told the police to stay with Husseini while I made a phone call. I reached the head of security, and told him about Husseini's antics with Muzinga. One of the policemen took the phone and was ordered to tell Husseini that reports had come in indicating that his enemies were after him and that he would therefore be put under "protective custody." The doctor objected strenuously as they escorted him to a Jeep.

Several weeks later I received a call from *la Soeur* Donatienne, a saintly nun in charge of the hospital pavilion that contained special rooms for prisoners and the insane. She told me that a doctor from Yemen, critically ill, had asked whether I would take care of him.

An MP let me into the room. Husseini was lying in bed on his back. I put my hand on his shoulder. He opened his eyes and said in a weak, shaky voice, "Thank you for coming, Doctor."

"I'm sorry to see you sick," I said, pulling up a chair.

He was deeply jaundiced and had the odor of a dying man. I slipped my hand down to his abdomen. His liver was huge and rock hard.

"I need someone to talk to," he whispered. "I know I am dying. I do not want to suffer. The pain and the itching are unbearable. Can you help me?"

"I will do what is necessary to ease your suffering," I replied. He closed his eyes; for a long time neither of us spoke. Then I said softly, "Look, Husseini, I don't know what your beliefs are, or where you think you are going when you die, but if you have anything to say I will listen. Do you need a Bible or a Koran?"

"Thank you, but all I need is to talk."

Some days later his liver cancer killed him. I know he died without pain. I think he died at peace knowing that his deathbed confession might see him to a better world.

He did not tell me where the treasure was hidden, but then, I did not ask him. I suppose only he and his gorilla-hormone patient knew its location, and by eliminating Muzinga, all the lucre would have been his. His part of the secret died with him.

CHAPTER 12

The Prince
and the Prisoner

M Y FIRST CONTACTS with the Congolese Army, aside from those in the operating room, took place through the efforts of Stéphane d'Arenberg of Belgium. D'Arenberg was a prince of royal blood as well as a doctor. He had been a public health officer in Ruanda-Urundi before coming to the Congo during the chaotic days following independence and the army mutiny. His mission was to get as many of his compatriots out of prison as he could.

I was operating on a wounded soldier one night when a noise from the screened-off terrace made me look up. A man wearing a gray wash-and-wear suit, a gray wash-and-wear tie, and a white wash-and-wear shirt stood at the door of the operating room. He was a big man, showing a middle-age spread. His large head was starting to bald and the wisps of hair on the top were in disarray. Sweat poured down his round face, and the collar and armpits of his jacket were wet and dark. He was obviously agitated and in a hurry.

"Are you the American doctor Bill Close?" he asked in heavily accented English.

"Yes."

"My name is d'Arenberg. I am a Belgian doctor. I must talk with you. Are you almost through?" He took a large white handkerchief out of his pocket and wiped off his face and the top of his head.

"Almost," I said. "What's the problem?"

"I cannot speak in front of them," he said, indicating the soldier on the table and Makila, almost asleep but faithfully squeezing the balloon of the anesthesia machine.

"The patient is asleep and Makila doesn't speak English—he hardly understands French. Go ahead, what can I do for you?" My hope was that he would tell me what he had to, then bug off. I was really tired and wanted to go home to bed.

D'Arenberg stepped into the operating room and, staying by the door, told me that he had just been to Luzumu on the outskirts of Léopoldville. Luzumu was a prison with a reputation for cruelty and violence unequaled by any of the others in the city. Rhinoceros-hide whips, the "*chicottes*" of the colonial period, chains, manacles, and other torture instruments were on display at the entrance for the benefit of inmates and visitors. Colonel Mobutu had arrested some of the more violent men around Lumumba and thrown them into Luzumu. D'Arenberg's mission was to see whether any Europeans were there as well. He found none, but he had been cornered in one of the larger cells by a half-dozen brutes loyal to Lumumba, who had threatened to cut his throat if he did not take a "certain prisoner" out with him "for medical treatment." D'Arenberg had consented. After a discussion with the prison guards, who were loyal to Mobutu, and the passage of a little "*matabish*" for beer and cigarettes, the "certain prisoner" was freed from the wires that bound his wrists to his ankles and thrown into the back of d'Arenberg's car. On the way into town, the doctor learned that the man riding away from Luzumu on his backseat was the infamous Fataki, one of Lumumba's most sadistic henchmen—a master of torture and slow death. D'Arenberg knew he would be in serious trouble if Mobutu found out Fataki had been released. His immediate concern was not only to deal with Fataki's "medical" problems, but also to hold him securely for the night.

I glanced at the prince as he finished his story. Sweat dripped from his chin and soaked his gray tie.

"Where is he now?" I asked, putting the last sutures in the soldier's abdominal wound.

"I put him on the X-ray table in your emergency room. He is complaining of back pain, which is quite likely after being trussed up like a chicken for God knows how long. I thought you could treat him and keep him overnight with a police guard."

"The police took off to fight against the army," I said. "We don't have any guards. As a matter of fact, we don't have any X-ray film." I pulled off my bloody gloves and soggy gown and looked at him. He smiled, shrugged his shoulders, and held out his hands in the European way that says silently and so eloquently, *"Eh bien, qu'est-ce que vous voulez? C'est comme ça*—Well, what do you expect? That's the way it is." I laughed and went over to him.

"Glad to meet you, Doctor," I said as we shook hands. Any man who was banging on the doors of local prisons in search of Europeans had my respect. He followed me to the X-ray room. On the table was Fataki, lying on his side with his knees up to his chin.

"Here is the doctor. He will take care of you," said d'Arenberg. Fataki showed me his wrists and ankles where wires had cut into the skin.

It was hard to feel sorry for Fataki. His own men had mistreated him; he had done much worse to others. I examined him. Aside from some bruises on his back and the wounds around his ankles and wrists, he had no other obvious injuries. I went through the motions of taking X rays with the empty cassettes and, after spending a few moments in the dark room, returned to the X-ray table.

Fataki was waiting expectantly. I told him that his back needed to be immobilized for a while to relieve him of his pain, and that the best way to do that would be to put him in a cast. He nodded. I pulled over the plaster cart and went to work. D'Arenberg took off his jacket, rolled up his sleeves, and helped. The next thing Fataki knew he was in a body spica—a plaster cast that went from his belly button to his knees with a hole cut out for toilet functions. I wrapped plaster around a broomstick and fixed it to the cast between his knees to help carry him. As the whole thing hardened, he realized that he was trapped. He was fatalistic about this turn of events and was silent as we loaded him back into d'Arenberg's car for the trip back to Luzumu.

Two nights later d'Arenberg returned in the same gray suit, still sweating. He had been manning the dispensary of the First Para-Commando Battalion in the camp where Colonel Mobutu had a house overlooking the Congo River. D'Arenberg had to return to Belgium right away and wanted to know if I would take on the medical responsibilities of the paratroopers and the colonel.

The next day we drove out to the camp and he introduced me briefly to Major Tshatshi, the battalion commander. That same day, after surgery, I returned in the evening for a longer talk with the major. It took some argument at the entrance of the camp before I was let in. Whites were suspect, and apparently the MPs at the gate had not been told of my new duties. I said, "*Ngai monganga na para*—I am the doctor for the paras," which reassured them. An MP climbed in and escorted me to the major's house. He indicated that I should stay in the car until he checked to see if I was expected. After a few minutes he returned to the car, opened the door, and led me into the house. He pointed to a chair in the living room and said, "*Tikala*—Wait."

Eight Congolese men and women sat silently in a circle, comfortably ensconced in deep armchairs and a large plush sofa. They stared at me. I had learned quickly that, as in Europe, one was expected to shake hands with everyone and say, "*Mbote*—Good day." I made the rounds and sat in an empty chair, hoping that I would not have to wait for all of them to be seen first. No one spoke. Some stared out of the window, others studied an old Flemish print of a buxom nude coyly peeking out from behind a bowl of ripe fruit. The heavy, elaborate frame hung above a dark piece of carved furniture. Before the army had taken over the camp, it had been the housing complex for junior colonial functionaries. The house in which Colonel Mobutu lived had belonged to a Belgian banker.

I offered comments about the heat and the weather, and asked those sitting near me about their families—the usual stuff. The replies were monosyllabic. It was clear that they did not want to talk. It seemed to me that they must be waiting to see the major about some tragedy.

After twenty minutes or more Major Tshatshi strode into the room. "*Mbote, Docteur,*" he said, shaking my hand. He turned to the others in the room. "*Monganga na biso*—Our doctor." He pointed to me, smiling. They acknowledged this with silent, serious nods. "*Viens, Docteur,*" he said. I followed him into his office. He pointed me to a chair and sat behind the desk.

"Nice to see you again," I said. "But before we start, can you tell me what has happened?"

"Nothing has happened that I know of. Why do you ask?"

"In the living room there are eight people sitting around in a circle, not talking. Not saying anything at all. Has someone died?"

The major laughed. "No one has died. Everything is

going well. I am glad you can come and take care of the dispensary."

"Thank you, Major." I persisted: "Why are the people sitting in a silent circle?"

"Maybe they have nothing to say for the moment," he replied gently. It was my turn to be silent.

Through the years, Tshatshi became a good friend. He and I, and an Israeli doctor, Dan Michaile, helped prepare the battalion for their jump training in Israel. That was before the Congo broke with the Israelis in the hope that they would get preferential treatment by the Arabs during the first oil crisis. We developed standards of health and physical fitness, and organized athletic competitions in soccer, boxing, and field events between the four companies that made up the battalion. "Paraball" was a noteworthy sport invented during that time. It was played on a soccer field with a large leather medicine ball that must have weighed twenty pounds. Whenever possible, the most important matches were played during torrential rainstorms, when the mud factor was at its best. There were ten men on a team and the ball was moved toward the enemy goal line by any means. There were no rules to limit fighting, charging, or any other form of conduct for that matter, except that the players had to stay within the confines of the field. There were few real injuries, probably because the mud acted as a lubricant and buffer between the players.

As the situation in the country improved, medical efforts expanded. Prince Stéphane d'Arenberg founded and led FOMETRO, *Fonds Médical Tropicale,* a nonprofit organization, into which he put a great deal of his own time and money. The organization that I started was the "little sister" of FOMETRO. It was called FOMECO, *Fonds Médical Congolais,* also a nonprofit organization that later ran the general hospital, the hospital riverboat, and the mother-child health centers in the slums of the capital. When Mobutu changed the name of the country from the Congo to Zaire, FOMECO became the *Fonds Médical de Coordination,* thus saving the money we would have spent on new letterheads. Stéphane and I saw each other every time he came to Africa, and I was occasionally his guest in Brussels.

After 1977, when I left Africa, we lost touch. Then, in 1985, he sent me a Christmas card from Cape Town. He wrote, "After a big heart operation in Switzerland I could return for the European winter to South Africa and summer. How are you doing? I have kept the greatest *souvenirs.*"

I answered with a long letter catching him up on my professional life and saying, "All our children and grandchildren are fine and doing well in their various fields of interest. Tine is well, and having fun raising *bouviers des Flandres,* those great shaggy dogs from your country. So you see, Stéphane, we still have some Flemish friends living with us. I also have wonderful memories from our time and work together. How we would love to see you again. I do remember the first time we met, at night, in the operating room."

The last word I had from d'Arenberg was at the end of January 1986. He wrote a short note from Cape Town. After thanking me for my letter, he said, "I want absolutely to keep in contact. Alas, I am, for the moment, very badly organized, but I would want that these few lines bring to you, without too much delay, my very sincere thanks, and the expression of all my friendship."

"Very badly organized" was the prince's euphemism for "very sick indeed." The next word I had was that he had returned to Switzerland and died unexpectedly. I, and many of us, had lost a courageous and generous colleague.

Stéphane d'Arenberg was a nobleman in the finest sense of the word.

Fataki, it was rumored, came to a soggy end at the hands of his own people, who had decided that enough was enough. He was again trussed up with wire like a chicken and thrown into the cataracts beyond the Stanley Pool.

Tshatshi later became a colonel and was in command of the 3rd Army Group in Stanleyville. In 1968, he was killed by mutinous troops who ambushed him at the entrance to his own camp as he was returning from an inspection of the town. The dissidents were part of a Katangese battalion that had rebelled against the central government in Léopoldville.

CHAPTER 13

The Delivery of the President's Cousin

ONE EVENING, after playing the agreed maximum of thirteen games of checkers, the president offered me a cognac. We sat on the terrace and watched the night take over the day across the rapids. "My cousin wants you to deliver her baby," he said.

"General," I said, "I don't know anything about delivering babies. I'll get the chief of our maternity service to attend her. He's a professor from Canada. He is very good and he's gentle. Your cousin will love him. You know we're averaging a hundred and twenty deliveries a day at the hospital," I added, sipping the brandy and trying to bring the subject to a close.

"She wants you there," said the president.

"I'll be glad to be around," I answered, "but I'll call the professor and ask him to do the delivery."

"That's fine, if you are there," he repeated firmly.

A few days later the call came. The cousin was having contractions every two minutes, and she had those ominous "bearing down" sensations. The professor had been primed for the occasion and was on his way to the hospital. Yes, yes, I would go, too.

When I got to the delivery room at the private hospital, the action had begun. The professor, a tall distinguished gentleman, was at the lower end of the table. He was gowned, gloved, and masked. He rested his right elbow on the cousin's knee as she relaxed between contractions.

"Hello, Dr. Close," he said. "We have been waiting for you."

"I'll bet you have," I said—my adrenals sending warning squirts throughout my body.

I took my station at the north end of the table and smiled weakly to the cousin.

"Ahhh, *Docteur,*" she said, digging her well-manicured fingernails into my upper arm. "I am so glad you are here."

A contraction came and her grip on my upper arm paralyzed my biceps, triceps, and all distal muscles and tissues.

Paulette, an enthusiastic and knowledgeable OB nurse, was at the cousin's side.

"Go 'hoo hoo hoo' when the contractions come," she said to the patient.

They both went "hoo, hoo, hoo" together as the next contraction took over.

"Now," said Paulette, every fiber of her system concentrated on the next phase of the action, "go *ahh, ahh, ahh* and relax."

During the hoo hoos and the ahh ahhs, I gathered from the professor's grunts of approval and gentle encouragement of the patient that the baby was working its way down the birth canal and that delivery was imminent. These events, taken with the noises coming from the cousin at the head of the table, contrived to decrease the blood and oxygen to my thalamus and cortex. This was compounded by the loss of all feeling in my left arm from the tourniquet effect of the cousin's fingernails. I grabbed the edge of the table with my free hand to keep from falling.

"Bill," said the professor, "maybe you'd better go and lie down somewhere. You look like hell."

I said, "Thanks, old buddy, I feel like hell."

I pried the cousin's fingers off my arm and staggered into the labor room next door. It was spotlessly clean. The bed had pure white sheets stretched without a wrinkle over the rubber mattress. I could not lie there; the head nursing sister would be outraged. So I crawled under the bed, on the cool linoleum floor, nun clean.

When I was flat on my back the blood returned to my head, the light-headedness faded, and the sweat lost its cold clinging quality with the return of some body heat. Just as I was beginning to feel normal again, I heard the Brunhild cry of the senior sister in maternity, "*Docteur Cloooose, Docteur Cloooose. Où est le Docteur Clooooose? On lui demand au téléphone.*" Probably the president wanting to know how his cousin was coming along.

No one knew where Dr. Close had gone.

As I lay under the bed I saw the senior sister's large ankles pass three feet from my face as she continued her clarion calls for me. She did not look under the bed. Her size would have precluded this maneuver, and I would like to think, it would not have occurred to her that the president's doctor would be on the floor in the labor room. As she departed, the echoes of her call faded down the hall.

I struggled back to my station at the head of the table in the delivery room. The cousin reapplied her viselike grip on my upper arm.

The situation still seemed far from resolution, but the professor said, with the gallantry and optimism that seemed to be part of his specialty, "Only a couple more pushes and we will have a baby." Paulette, her face red with exertion, sweat pouring off her brow, urged the lady into the last few pushes, and the baby came quietly and with dignity, emitting a lusty cry as he took his first breath. We'd been four, now we were suddenly five.

CHAPTER 14

The Mango Kid

I HAD STOPPED LISTENING to local radio broadcasts: the charges and countercharges made me nervous. But I understood the reason politicians and plotters of coups went for radio stations like mad dogs go for the throat. Those who control the flow of news and propaganda control the population.

Ghanaian United Nations troops were dug in around the buildings of the Congolese National Radio. Lumumba, the prime minister, arrived with two truckloads of loyal soldiers and threatened to shoot his way in. Colonel Aferi, a Sandhurst-trained officer in charge, marched up to the lead vehicle, pointed to the line of blue helmets and weapons peeking through a trench, and shook his head. Furious, Lumumba ordered his troops to attack. Seeing that they were dangerously exposed, Lumumba's men refused to obey and retreated. These events were reported to us by Colonel Aferi himself, who arrived, a little late, for a long-standing lunch date right after the confrontation.

So Lumumba, the Congolese prime minister (or ex–prime minister, depending on who you listened to) was now under house arrest on the orders of President Kasa Vubu, whose authority he had tried to revoke. Had it not been for the people maimed or killed in the streets and bars of Léopoldville by the recurrent fighting between the army and the police, and the tribal brawls between machete-wielding Bakongo and Bayaka, the situation would have been an *opéra bouffe*. Lumumba's residence was guarded by a company of Ghanaians who were themselves surrounded by anti-Lumumba Congolese soldiers who were sure the pro-Lumumba United Nations troops would smuggle him out of the capital to Stanley-ville, his northeastern stronghold.

In the hospital, driblets of news came from the wounded, or from zealous foreign reporters who wanted body counts on the battered or dead. From dawn to late at night Sister Germaine, the OR crew, and I sewed, debrided, reduced fractures, extracted lead slugs, and pronounced dead the remains of what had been human beings.

One afternoon I was finishing up on a paratrooper with a bullet wound in his abdomen—my tenth major operation of the day. The bullet had struck the man in the lower left chest, perforated his stomach twice, chewed up his left kidney and spleen, and put a couple of holes in his gut before lodging in his back muscles. Since we didn't find the bullet and there was no wound of exit, I assumed it must be in there somewhere. We still had no X-ray film. The soldier was in shock and unconscious. After opening his abdomen wide and sucking out the blood, I removed what was left of his spleen. His left kidney was too damaged to leave in—luckily, the right one felt normal. I controlled the bleeding and sewed up the holes in his bowel and stomach. His pressure came up and he started to groan and move as we placed the drains and fixed the final wire sutures in his abdominal wall. I would have given him blood if we'd had any. We didn't even have a lab.

During the surgery the soldier's buddies barged into the operating room with their guns. One of them, a huge sergeant, snarled that if the man died we would be shot. Sister Germaine spun around in her blood-soaked blouse and, with gloved hands on her hips, shouted that if they didn't get out of the OR we would stop working. The sergeant took a step toward her and growled something in Lingala. She shook a bloody finger at him and pointed to the door, as you would to a dog who had just peed on the carpet. "*Kende—sortez, sortez,*" she yelled, and stamped her feet to get the soldiers moving faster. They left muttering, "*Sales Flamands.*" Tough lady, that sister!

After we were through, I walked into the little office between the OR and the sterilizer room to add the soldier's name and what we had done to him to the register. Pierre, the OR orderly, came to tell me that another patient had been brought in. I stood up, stretched, and followed him out to where a boy lay on a gurney.

Apparently he and his friends had been plucking mangoes in one of the big trees that lined the road to Binza, when a branch snapped and he had fallen. A crowd had quickly gathered, and an officer, who was passing by in his Jeep, had picked him up and brought him to the hospital. The policeman knew nothing about the boy's background and assumed he was one of many abandoned children who attach themselves loosely to families living in the slums. These waifs foraged in garbage cans or begged for leftovers and, during the mango season, lived off the fruit they sold by the roadside. Unlike many thin, potbellied children who suffered from chronic protein deficiency, this boy looked healthy—a survivor. I washed the plaster off my hands and stepped over to the table. The sister came in and grumbled about a dirty child on the clean sheet.

The boy was drowsy and groaned as he rocked his head slightly from side to side. His blood pressure and pulse were normal. He winced when I touched a swelling above his right ear. His pupils reacted equally to light and were in the midposition. Although there was a little blood in his nose, he had no blood or liquid behind his eardrums. His neck and limbs checked out well, and he raised his arms and legs and stuck out his tongue when I asked him to. All his reflexes were normal.

We had run out of X-ray film again, so we had no way of getting more specific about his head injury except by watching him carefully. He certainly had a concussion, but whether he was bleeding inside his skull we might not know for a while. I sat at the head of the table with his head cradled in my palms. Poor little tyke. There was red sand in his short black hair and eyebrows. His chest rose and fell gently as he breathed, no problem there; his lungs were clear, his tummy soft and flat. Peeking from the right pocket of his khaki shorts was the tip of a green mango.

I sat and watched. The sister brought a basin of soapy water to clean him up. She started with the dried blood and dirt in his nose. Then, with a finger poked into a cloth, she washed his ears, carefully removing the grit from the little caves and crevices in the front of the ear flaps. She cleaned the inner angles of his eyes with wet cotton, then took off his shorts and washed and dried the rest of his body. When she was through I asked her to put his pants back on—I was worried that his mango would disappear.

"Do you know his name?" she asked.

"No. The police didn't say." We looked down at him.

"Good-looking little boy," she said. "Let's call him Patrice."

Every fifteen minutes I checked his vital signs and level of consciousness. They were steady. He remained drowsy but obeyed commands when aroused. His pupils showed no changes.

The sister rearranged my schedule for the rest of the afternoon so I could watch the boy without interruption and be free to act if necessary. Patients who had lined up outside the door for surgical consultations were told to

return in the morning. Some who had come from far away
sat on benches outside or slept next to a bundle of
personal effects under the trees next to the building. They
lay on the grass, keeping the covered walkways free for
the constant traffic of patients and sisters.

I continued at the head of the table, my arms resting
on a pillow. The child's quiet, steady breathing was
making me sleepy. I thought of another boy about the
same age who had been playing in the street with his
friends. A spent bullet had dropped into his open mouth
as he looked up to catch a ball. He had been admitted to
my service with this unbelievable story, proven true when
I took out a jagged piece of lead the size of a lima bean
from under his tongue, which, amazingly, was untouched.
He had neither resisted nor cried. His name was Antoine.
I kept him in the hospital for a week of antibiotics.

I thought about the infant who had been rushed in a
few days ago with stab wounds in the chest and abdomen.
The baby was a victim of a wild fight in a bar. I had just
concluded that he was dead when the father, screaming
hysterically, rushed into the operating room and snatched
the little body away. Carrying it high over his head, he
barged through the crowd around the hospital entrance
and ran out into the street.

We dealt with a lot of trauma: heads bashed in by gun
butts and police clubs; deep slashes from machetes that
came near to severing arms and legs; and stab wounds
from bayonets and knives. One man was flown in from
the interior with an arrow in his chest. The feathered shaft
had penetrated next to his right nipple; the metal tip
poked out from his shoulder blade. I cut off the shaft and
pulled the arrow through; he recovered. Many came in
with bullet wounds, some from lead balls fired from
muzzle-loaded "poopoo" guns used in the bush by
hunters. A fisherman who had fallen out of his pirogue

was rushed in by his friends almost dead from loss of blood. His genitals and part of his groin had been bitten off by a crocodile.

I thought about Jerome, a soldier with his chin blown away. Only small fragments of jawbone remained on each side of his face, and what was left of his tongue was peppered with bone spicules. Since there were no maxillofacial or plastic surgeons in the country, I did the best I could. I put him to sleep with a tube through his nose into his trachea, then cleaned him up, squirting buckets of saline into the mangled remains of his lower face. I cut the dead tissue from his tongue and picked out the bone fragments. After excising both iliac crests—the bony ridges on each side of his pelvis—we wired them together, then wired the new "chin bone" to what was left of his jaw. I pulled a skin flap up from his neck to help close the lower aspect of the wound. Two weeks later he developed infection around some of the wires but was healing, and was already getting used to having his wife grind up all his food.

I raised my head . . . must have dozed off. Something was different. I looked at the boy: his head was turned to the right, his breathing slow and deep. His right pupil was huge, the left small. Both eyes stared fully to the right and slightly up. I could not arouse him, but his right arm and leg moved sluggishly when I pinched them. His left side was flaccid and did not respond at all to any painful stimuli. I ran my thumbnail up the soles of his feet. On the left his great toe pulled back like a hitchhiker's thumb. I called out to the OR boys. Makila shuffled in, dragging his mop.

"Get the sister, quickly," I told him. He dropped the mop handle and scurried out. Moments later *Soeur* Germaine came running in followed by Pierre.

"I think this kid's just localized his injury. Check his pressure."

She pumped up the sleeve. "Hundred and fifty over a hundred." Then: "Pulse only forty-eight."

"The pressure in his head is going up." I closed my eyes. Only once before had I faced this situation, as a resident at the Roosevelt. A calm neurosurgeon had talked me through the procedure. This kid must have just bled into his subdural or epidural space. Which one? At this point did it matter? The only thing that might save him was a burr hole through the skull to relieve the pressure of the blood on his brain. But where do I drill the hole? *The eyes gaze toward the lesion,* sounded somewhere in my memory. *Go in where a line from the eyebrow meets a line coming up from the ear.*

"Do we have a trephine—something to make a burr hole?"

"I don't think so." She hurried into the instrument room and returned, shaking her head.

"Run over to the carpentry shop and get a brace and bit. Maybe that'll work," I said. She sailed out of the veranda door, white skirts and headgear flying.

By the time she returned with the tools, Pierre and I had shaved the hair off the area to be opened and washed it with soap and water. The boy's respirations remained deep and slow. I put an airway in his mouth, then incised the scalp down to the skull with one stroke. We controlled the bleeding with finger pressure on the lips of the wound. The brace and bit, which the sister had wiped off with alcohol, worked well, and I was quickly through the outer plate. Then we advanced slowly, the sister washing away the shavings and soft fragments of cortical bone with squirts of saline from a large bulb syringe. A little more, then just a little more, and the bottom of the hole turned blue. With a bone snip, I carefully enlarged the hole, then with the tip of a scalpel picked away the final layer to expose the dura, the tough fibrous membrane covering the brain; it bulged into the hole. I nicked it and dark blood spurted. Within seconds they boy's eyes were centered, his pupils equal in size. He awoke and struggled to sit.

After that we kept him in P1, where "miscellaneous" children with chronic diseases and a few kids with no place to go were housed. I showed him off to friends and visitors. That primitive procedure was the apogee of my surgical career. I felt wonderfully fulfilled.

After Patrice had recovered from his primitive craniotomy, he would stand outside the veranda and watch me operate. When he arrived at his station each morning he greeted me with a "*Mbote, nganga*—Hello, healer," and I replied "*Mbote, mwana kitoko*—Hello, handsome child." Then he'd settle in and follow the action in the OR.

During those weeks I kept a log of the number of various operations I did from July 10 to September 28:

Gastrectomy	1
Laminectomy	1
Nephrectomy	1
Appendectomy	17
Open reduction of femur fracture with Kuntchner nailing	10
Thoracotomy for bullet wound	1
Inguinal herniorraphy:	
a. simple	72
b. incarcerated	8
Debridement, fracture femur and bullet wound	1
Finger amputation	7
Open reduction fracture radius	1
Excision olecranon bursa	1

Below-knee amputation	1
Open reduction both bones of forearm	3
Laparotomy:	
a. Diffuse peritonitis from perforated appendix	1
b. Stab wound	1
c. Pregnancy	1
d. Peritonitis from rupture amebic abscess	1
e. Tuberculous peritonitis	2
f. Splenectomy for ruptured spleen	1
g. Mesenteric adenitis	1
External fixation of fractured jaw	4
Albee fusion for tuberculosis of spine	3
Hemorrhoidectomy	14
Open reduction of fracture of humerus	3
Resection of traumatic aneurysm neck from stab wound	1
Colon resection for volvulus with gangrene	3
Cholecystectomy	1
Open reduction of tibial fracture with Kuntchner nailing	2
Extraction bullets	5
Debridement bullet wounds	3
Fistula in ano	1
Incision and drainage of liver abscess (2 liters of pus)	1
Skin grafts	3
Fixation sternoclavicular subluxation	1
Prostatectomy	1
Amputation of penis for cancer	1
Smith-Peterson nailing of hip fracture	1
Resection of osteoma from femur	1
Perifemoral sympathectomy	1
Bone graft for pseudoarthosis both bones of forearm	1

Reduction of ileo-cecal intussusception in
    infant   1
Repair of harelip   1
Enucleation of eye   2
Achilles tendon lengthening for polio
    contracture   3
Cystostomy for removal of stone and
    obstruction   2
Kirshner wirings of fractured clavicle   2
Excision fibula sequestration in infant with
    sickle-cell anemia   1

Not long after Patrice recovered, I received letters from Moral Re-Armament Headquarters urging me to stop operating and return to the pulpit, so to speak. After much soul-searching I determined to follow my own vocation and slowly their control over me subsided.

CHAPTER 15

The Boy with the Broken Leg

HE WAS IN HIS EARLY TEENS, dressed in a white T-shirt and khaki shorts, both smeared with dirt from the accident. He lay sweating and rigid with fear, gripping his left thigh. Sister Germaine, in her usual brusque way, snatched the boy's hands off his leg and placed them firmly on either side of his body, commanding him not to move. The boy clenched his teeth and grabbed the rubber sheet but lay still.

I patted his shoulder. "*Nkombo na yo*—What is your name?"

"*Kumu*, Albert," he whispered.

"*Kobanga te*—Don't be frightened," I said. He nodded and closed his eyes tightly.

He had a small gash in his leg, about halfway between the knee and ankle. Dark blood, carrying tiny globules of fat, oozed from the wound. The leg was swollen and slightly angled outward. I touched the area around the laceration and felt the grinding movement of fragments under my fingers. The pulses in his ankle and foot were strong. It would have been nice to have an X ray.

The sister wheeled him into the operating room, and with Pierre steadying the injured leg, we lifted him off the gurney and onto the table. The boy put his hand over his mouth to stifle a cry, and tears squeezed out of his eyes, streaking the dirt on his face.

I pulled the anesthesia machine over, started an IV, and gave him some pentothal. He relaxed, blinked, and with a deep sigh went to sleep. Makila placed a mask over the boy's face. I adjusted the oxygen and nitrous-oxide knobs on the machine and Makila pushed on the balloon.

Sister Germaine brought warm, soapy water and a nailbrush whose bristles were worn and flat. She put on gloves and started to scrub the wound and leg. I went to the basin in the corner of the room to wash my hands. I was tired and the muscles in my shoulders ached; I did some shoulder shrugs and stretched my neck. I still had to drive to the paratrooper camp and see what they had in the dispensary before heading home to bed.

The sister finished prepping the leg, sloshed iodine and alcohol over the wound, and covered it with a sterile towel. She laid out what we would need on the instrument table. I picked up the gown, opened it, and pushed my hands through the sleeves; it was still damp. Something was wrong with the sterilizer.

We debrided the wound, and with Pierre pulling on the leg, the fragments slipped into place. When he released the traction, the ends of the bones locked into each other, and the reduction was maintained. I brought the skin edges together with stainless-steel sutures, then fluffed up gauze compresses to cover the wound and put on a light dressing and a thin, loose shell of plaster wrapped from the base of his toes to the upper thigh. As the plaster was hardening, the boy woke up. With the fracture set and immobilized, he had very little pain.

By the time I was through, the boy's father had arrived and was standing at the veranda door. I let him in, we shook hands, and he thanked me warmly for taking care of his son. He was a clerk in a bank, quiet and well educated. I told him about his son's injury and said that if the wound did not get infected he would do well, adding that we would have to keep him in the hospital for a couple of weeks.

I showered, put on street clothes, and drove to the paratrooper camp. After jabbing penicillin into a few soldiers with gonorrhea and splinting a broken finger, I went home. Trooper, my old black Lab, was there to greet me, and although I missed them, I was relieved that Tine and the kids were in Switzerland. It would have been nerve-racking to have them here in the middle of all the insecurity and chaos.

The next morning when I arrived at the hospital, Sister Euphrasie, who ran the surgical pavilions, met me at the door. She had found the boy in bad shape when she came on duty and asked me to follow her to P6.

Sitting by the bed, looking worried and tired, was the boy's father. I shook his hand, then took the boy's: it was hot and sweaty. He looked sick and had the red, dry eyes and dilating nostrils of someone feverish with a toxic infection. His toes, poking out of the plaster shell, were swollen and blue. The cast had become a tourniquet overnight. I opened it along the top and spread the edges. I watched the toes, expecting them to return to a healthy pink—they didn't. Cutting into the cast padding, I pulled away the dressings. They were fouled with a gray, putrid exudate. I pressed the dusky skin next to the wound; it felt like a sponge. Although I had never seen gas gangrene before, the smell and the feel were unmistakable. I cut off the top of the whole cast, dressed the wound, and asked the sister to give him three million units of penicillin every four hours. Then I sat on a corner of the bed and explained to the boy and his father that the cast I had put on to immobilize the fragments had not allowed for the swelling that developed during the night; now there was a serious infection. I had every hope that the antibiotics would help. I would check him again in the evening.

All through the day I found myself regretting that I had not left the wound open with the leg resting in a partial cast. The organism that causes gangrene does not grow well in fresh air.

That evening the leg seemed about the same, but the boy's pulse and temperature were going up: a bad sign. I walked outside with the father, and we sat on a bench near the OR.

"I must tell you," I began, "that if the infection does not come under control by tomorrow morning, I will have to amputate your boy's leg to save his life."

The father looked stunned, then buried his face in his hands. That night I hardly slept and left before dawn to see the boy.

Sister Euphrasie and I peeled off the dressings, and even before the wound was exposed, the fetid smell of wet gangrene banished any expectation that penicillin would be enough. Gray ooze seeped through the gauze. The gas had pushed farther up the leg, and the redness and swelling had progressed to a handbreadth below the knee. The boy had little pain—the nerves were destroyed. His fever was very high. I covered the wound and sat next to the bed. He glanced at me, then looked up at Sister Euphrasie, who stood on the other side with her hand on his shoulder. I stepped to the door and asked his father to come in. He stood opposite the sister and held his son's hand. I told the boy that I had to take him back to the operating room and put him to sleep again and take off his leg. He cried out, *"Non,"* and his father hugged him tightly. I added that if I operated now, I thought we could save his knee. His father looked at me steadily for a moment, then lowered his head to hide the tears that welled up and ran down his cheeks.

He said quietly, "Do whatever you think is necessary."

Sister Germaine cradled his head in her hands as I put him to sleep. I did a guillotine amputation, leaving the wound open because of the infection. After the operation

I found the father sitting on the bench under the palm tree next to the OR. I sat next to him. We didn't talk for a while. Then I turned to him.

"I will have the best artificial leg available in the United States sent to your boy every year until he finishes growing."

"You can do that?"

"Yes."

We stood, and he embraced me. We both wept. I walked him back to his son's bedside and left them together.

In the shower, I scrubbed away the sweat and stains of surgery, then dressed and slipped out the back door. I walked to the small Catholic chapel around the corner. The priest, a hospital chaplain and friend, had shown me the loose brick behind which he hid the key to the vestry. The morning service had just ended. The fragrance of candles and incense lingered—a welcome contrast to the smells of the OR. I slipped into the front pew and sat staring at the altar, but all I saw was the amputated leg. Would the boy have developed gangrene with a different dressing? Who knows? I felt overwhelmed by the cost to this father and son of a cast I put on too tight. Quitting surgery was a temptation. I could go away . . . do something else where the stakes were not so high. Had I been too cocky after saving Patrice? Probably. Was the tragedy retribution for turning my back on "God's Will" according to the directors of Moral Re-Armament? Surely a loving God would not be party to such a thing. The pressure from some of the leaders in Moral Re-Armament had grown steadily. I was urged to return to the fold, to stop operating, do more proselytizing, return to what they called my "manifest destiny." I resisted the idea, and yet, had the boy with the broken leg been the victim of my resistance to MRA's idea of God's will for my life? I looked around the chapel and slowly doubts were replaced by peaceful resolve. By focusing on what they termed sinful ambition and the big "I," MRA was trying to pry me loose from a profession that had been a vocation from my earliest years. Some people may be destined to be priests or proselytizers, but not me.

After a while I left and walked slowly to my car, parked behind the surgical buildings. As I approached, a small boy stepped out from the shadows with his hand outstretched.

"*Mbote, nganga,*" said Patrice, holding up a large golden mango.

"*Mbote, mwana kitoko,*" I replied, kneeling down to take him and his mango in my arms.

I drove home. The night watchman asked me whether it was true that Lumumba had escaped from the city and was heading toward Stanleyville. I confirmed this with a telephone call. More killings, more misery for this shattered country.

CHAPTER 16

Tata Felix

ARLY IN 1961, the Congo was still making headlines in the international press. In February, when news of Lumumba's murder was flashed around the world, mobs in Cairo ransacked the Belgian Embassy. In Paris, African students demonstrated against the presence of Belgian troops in the Congo. Those of us in Léopoldville wondered anxiously what would happen next. By March, Katanga's President Tshombe was under house arrest in the paratrooper camp.

I had met Colonel Mobutu a month or so earlier when I was called to his house to pull a fish bone out of his great-aunt's throat. I could just see the tip of the bone peeking over the crest of her tongue. Grateful for the stroke of luck that made it visible, I pulled it out with a clamp. Mobutu thanked me and I left.

A few days later I was summoned again. This time he asked me to see another aunt, who was at home and very sick. He ordered one of his aides to show me where she lived. After a long drive into the heart of the *cité Africaine,* we pulled up to a small, neat house surrounded by a fenced yard of packed dirt. Half a dozen people sat around a charcoal fire. My guide told them I was a doctor sent by Colonel Mobutu. I shook hands all around and was ushered into the house, down a tiny corridor, and into a small room where a dozen people crowded around a canvas cot on which lay an ancient, skeletal woman almost completely covered by mothballs. Again, I made the rounds shaking hands then squatted next to the patient. Her crescendo-diminuendo breathing indicated

118

that she did not have long to live. I examined her briefly, then stood up and announced the obvious, "She is not suffering." I bowed slightly to the gathering and left. An hour later I was standing in front of Mobutu.

"I saw your aunt, Colonel. I'm afraid she is dying."

"I know that," he replied. "The family was with her?"

"Yes. The room was packed with people."

"How long did you stay?"

"Oh, I suppose ten or fifteen minutes."

"Please return to the house and sit with her longer. It will comfort the family."

I returned to the small house and learned the meaning and value of an *acte de présence*.

Now a message was delivered by an MP: a request for a house call on the colonel's "visitor," who turned out to be Tshombe. He was apparently nervous and having trouble sleeping. After a brief medical check I gave him a mild sedative, brought him some books and magazines, and made sure his food was adequate.

At home we were having our own nervous nights. I resisted the idea of a guard until our house was burglarized for the third time. Thieves came right into the bedroom as we were sleeping. My wife, Tine, who was over on a short visit, had her camera and purse stolen; they took my medical bag and Zenith shortwave radio. Between our beds they left a large rock, probably to use on our heads if we had awakened.

A week after Tine flew back to Switzerland to join the children, a black car cruised around the house and someone tossed a brick into the yard with a note saying, "We reserve for you a special ending." I drove to the paratrooper camp and asked Major Tshatshi to recommend a man I could hire as a night watchman.

Early the next morning a sergeant arrived at the house

with Tata Felix, a tall, thin Bangala—the warrior tribe from the north. His bearing was military, and the tribal markings across his forehead gave him a fearsome, distinguished look. He carried a spear and wore a faded khaki tunic with medals dangling from the pocket. The sergeant told me that the old man had served in the Belgian Colonial Brigade during World War I. We offered him a small cash salary and set up his routine. He was to arrive at sunset and leave at dawn and would receive a loaf of bread and a large mug of strong tea and milk laced with three tablespoons of sugar. If he wanted peanuts, he would bring them.

Tata Felix showed up that same evening, and from then on the ritual was the same. He banged on the door, and when one of us opened it, he snapped to attention and saluted. After leaning his spear against the wall, he took the mug and bread and placed them carefully on the low wall separating the porch from the garden. Then he dunked the bread into the brew and gummed down the soggy mixture.

Tata's guard post was a broken-down armchair on the porch. A tattered cushion gave the seat a little extra padding as its springs had long since pushed through the webbing. The old soldier ate peanuts from a small brown paper bag he pulled out of his pocket, dropping the shells onto the tiled floor. He seemed to delight in crushing under his thick, callused heel the ants and cockroaches attracted by the hulls.

During the following months we had peaceful nights, except for the telephone. I had to admit that the presence of Tata Felix on the porch seemed to discourage the thieves, even though, as far as I could tell, the old man slept in the chair most of the night with his spear leaning against the wall. When I was called to the hospital, I would go out and come back in quietly so as not to disturb him. But once, as I struggled out of bed at two in the morning, I woke him up.

"Tata, how can you protect us if you sleep all night?" I asked him, with some heat.

He opened one eye. "I am here. No thieves have come." He tucked himself deeper into the chair as I drove out of the yard.

Early one morning, as I was finishing breakfast, Tata Felix banged on the door. I went to him, he saluted, and said, "*Yo yaku na ndako na ngai. Tala mwasi na ngai*—You come to my house. See my wife."

I looked at my watch, pointed to it, and shook my head. "No time before hospital," I told him.

He turned on his heel and walked down the steps to the car. After putting his spear in the back, he opened the passenger's door and sat down without a word.

"Hey, get out of there. I don't have time now," I shouted.

He didn't budge—just sat looking straight ahead. Damn. No use. I stomped back into the house, grabbed my bag and half-finished cup of coffee, and walked around to the driver's side. Tata leaned over and opened the door from the inside.

"Thanks a lot," I said, thoroughly annoyed by the old man. I put my bag in the back next to his spear, got in, slammed the door, and off we went. Quicker to go than to argue.

I pulled out of the drive, made two quick left turns, and took a right onto the city's main boulevard. The morning traffic was still light. The old man smelled of musty dust and charcoal fires; not as pungent as white body odor. I glanced at him; his eyes were fixed on the road. I opened the window and let the fresh morning air come in. A thunderstorm had crashed through the city during the night. In a few hours it would be sweltering.

The city of Kinshasa sprawled over thirty square miles from the river to the hills—most of it slums. Almost a million people lived there.

At the center of town, we turned right just before the post office, drove past the general hospital where I was supposed to start operating in half an hour, and continued for fifteen minutes into the slums, dodging kids, chickens, pigs, and old men straining in the head harnesses of carts loaded with everything and anything.

Tata directed me with grunts and finger pointing. We skirted piles of garbage and bounced along slowly through deep mud holes. We splashed through an open sewer and came to a stop at the end of a track next to a shack made of concrete blocks with a corrugated roof. Tata Felix opened his door and shooed away the scrawny children who had suddenly appeared. I stepped out with my black bag.

The old man pulled open a wooden door and motioned me to go in. The shack was dimly lit and ventilated through hollow bricks between the rough siding of the walls and the tin roof. Transparent little lizards scampered along the beams, aroused by the change in light as we walked in. In the center of the room, on a dirt floor swept smooth and clean, stood an ancient wooden table and two straight-backed chairs. Next to a wall a bed of planks was set on blocks and there, on a thin mat, an old woman lay on her side, her knees pulled up to her chin like a fetus. I left my bag on the table and approached her.

"*Mbote,* Mama," I said in greeting. No answer. I put my hand on her shoulder, squeezed it lightly, and repeated, "*Mbote,* Mama." No response. She was comatose. I glanced at Tata Felix. He looked down at his feet and said nothing.

I stepped back to the table, opened my bag, and took

out a stethoscope and blood-pressure cuff. Her pulse was slow and steady, but her pressure was high. I checked her eyes, and listened to her heart and lungs. Gently, I tried to extend her limbs and roll her onto her back so I could palpate her abdomen. I could not straighten her out. Amazingly, she had no bedsores. It seemed to me she must have had a stroke.

As I stuffed my things back in the bag, I thought, I must do something for this old woman. I wanted Tata Felix to think of me as a good doctor.

Many Africans feel they have not been treated properly unless they get a shot, preferably a painful one. So I drew up some vitamin B complex . . . at least a harmless placebo. I pulled back the cloth and wiped off her hip with an alcohol sponge. As the needle went in she moved a little to avoid the pain and let out a groan. "Ohooooo!"

Tata Felix shouted, "What did you do to her?"

I replied as I dropped the syringe into my bag, "I gave her a shot."

"*Mpo na nini*—What for?" he asked. He was angry. I was stunned and embarrassed. The Africans accepted almost any medical care without question, and gratefully at that.

"Why did you insist I come?" I asked, going on the attack.

He said nothing for a moment, then quietly he replied: "I wanted you to see her before she died. I did not think you would hurt her." He stepped over to the bed and looked down at the old woman. He put his hand on her head. "I asked you to come and be with her so I could tell our grandchildren a doctor had visited their dying parent." He looked up at me. "I did not think you would hurt her."

I closed my bag and went to the door, then turned to

glance back at the old couple. Tata Felix had pulled a chair over to the bed. He sat, shaking his head slowly and sadly. My heart ached. I felt empty and humiliated, and as I let myself out I wondered whether I would ever learn the complex art of medicine.

Tata Felix never returned to our porch. I carry his lesson for the rest of my life.

CHAPTER 17

Patrice and the Chimp

SOMETIMES HAPPY, refreshing events occurred to brighten what were otherwise days filled with pain and unpredictable chaos.

One morning I arrived in the operating room to find *Soeur* Germaine waiting at the door. "The mother superior wants to see you," she announced.

"Why? What for? Is there something wrong?" I asked. Command appearances, coming unexpectedly, always make my stomach tighten. Was there another crisis—another emergency about to hit us?

"How should I know why the reverend mother wants to see you?" she snapped. "Maybe she hasn't forgiven you and the children for your behavior last week. Anyway, you have half an hour before the first operation. I'll get things ready." I walked into the dressing room. As I stripped off my street clothes and pulled on OR greens and a white coat, I recalled last week's "military exercise" with the kids.

It was the mother superior's habit to emerge from the door between the convent and the hospital at precisely seven A.M., as regular as the rising sun. She was a large but well-proportioned and dignified woman who could, on occasion, be terrifying. When she glided along the covered walkways that connected the pavilions in the hospital, she was always gracious, greeting workers with a slight tilt of the head and raising of the hand like England's queen mother. No one would have tried to stop her when she was under way. Her large white headgear was the bow wave of a frigate under full steam. I watched her in awe, yet was tempted to test her serenity.

Early one morning I gathered together some of the boys in the convalescent pavilion adjacent to the trauma ward. Antoine and Patrice were the *capitas* or leaders of the little group. After swearing them to secrecy, I revealed my plot to ambush the mother superior as she entered the hospital for her morning rounds. I directed each one to a hiding place behind the palms and the big mango tree by their pavilion, then retreated to my own position behind a screen on the veranda off the operating rooms. From my "battle station," I could see both the door in the wall and the boys peeking around the trees. My signal for the attack was the flourishing of a bone saw, the nearest thing to a sword available. When the "sword" waved, they were to jump out at the reverend mother, yelling like banshees. We practiced the signal and the attack twice, and by that time it was 6:45. During the next fifteen minutes the children tittered and cringed behind the trees.

At seven A.M. sharp, the door opened, and the mother superior cruised majestically into the hospital. I waved the bone saw, and the kids charged her, screaming at the top of their lungs. The reverend mother sailed on with no acknowledgment of surprise but veered smoothly toward the operating room and, slowing briefly in front of me, declared, "Such tricks, *Docteur,* do not encourage good behavior in the children." Then bearing off to starboard, she headed for her office.

During the rest of the morning the happy, expectant faces of "my troops" were squeezed against the veranda mosquito netting, watching me attack the operating schedule for the day. At noon, I had the children line up, stand at attention, and salute as the reverend mother swept by on her way to the convent for lunch. At the door she turned and waved her hand.

"Good children," she said, including me in her

benevolence. That had been a week ago.

I walked to the superior's office two pavilions away, knocked, and entered. She was sitting at her desk.

"Ah, *Monsieur le docteur,* come in."

"Good morning, *ma mère*. You sent for me?"

"Yes. Please sit down. Do you know a little boy in P1 called Patrice?"

"Yes, very well. A sharp little rascal."

"I am worried about him. The sister in his pavilion tells me that every morning his shirt is torn, and he is covered with grime. Apparently, he goes out after dark when he should be sleeping. We cannot keep him in the ward in spite of threats of punishment. I told the mother of the night to tie him to his bed, but that did not work either. He is becoming a problem. We cannot continue to give him a new shirt every day. What do you think we ought to do with him?"

"He should have been discharged weeks ago, but we have no place to send him; he is an orphan." I thought for a moment. "Why not assign one of the young Congolese nuns to watch him? When he sneaks out, she can tail him at a distance."

What follows is the story we got the next day.

Around ten, when the hospital was asleep and the whole city had fallen quiet except for barking dogs, Patrice rolled out of bed. He had on a clean pair of khaki shorts and a short-sleeve, V-neck khaki shirt. After checking the walkways for the patrolling night *mère*, he skittered down the open corridor to the center of the hospital. Then, turning right, he headed for the door in the wall separating the maternity division from the rest of the pavilions. Opening it very carefully, he stuck his head through. Seeing that the way was clear, he ran the remaining thirty yards to the back entrance of the hospital and squeezed himself against the wall, looking around to

see if he had been followed. The Congolese nun darted
behind a post.

Slowly, with skill developed from climbing mango
trees, he went up the wall and dropped to the other side.
The nun ran to the lattice gate and watched while the
child strolled into the city zoo, which was adjacent to the
hospital's back wall. Only a few lights were burning
between the animal compounds, and for a moment she
lost him. Then she saw the boy approach a clearing under
a lamp hanging from a wire stretched between two palm
trees. He walked to the edge of the light and stopped. In
the center of the illuminated circle, an old chimpanzee,
crouching next to an iron stake, lifted his head and leaned
forward, balancing on his knuckles. Then, with one hand,
he reached up and eased the weight of a heavy steel collar
and chain off his shoulders. The boy and the ape stood
frozen and silent, each staring at the other without the
blinking of an eye. The nun behind her post held her
breath, fearing for the boy's life.

After a moment the chimp pushed out his lips and
bared his teeth in a grin. Patrice imitated him. The ape,
keeping the collar off his shoulders, bounced up and
down, hooting softly. The boy hopped from one foot to
the other, flexed elbows pressed to his ribs, hands and
head swinging from side to side. The chimp and the child
were in a world of their own, bound by the contact of
their eyes and the rhythmic synchrony of their bodies.
Patrice added a skip to each hop, and his body swayed as
he zigzagged slowly toward the ape, who, calling softly,
approached the boy in little jumps, the chain links
jangling in time with his movements. They watched each
other as the space between them narrowed, and as they
danced, puffs of dust kicked up by their feet rose in the
cone of light above their circular stage. Their music was
the patter of feet, the clinking chain, and the ape's soft

hooting. They continued like this for several minutes. Then, when the distance between them had narrowed to a few feet, the boy threw himself at the chimp, and they came together in a hug. After rolling over and over toward the stake, they sat each with his arm around the shoulders of the other.

For a long time the boy squatted with his back to the ape, who searched his dusty hair for mites and bugs. Then the chimp lay down and rested his head on the boy's knee as Patrice picked through the dark fur with the same care. Beyond the circle of light, a night bird cried, and dogs abandoned by owners who had fled during the troubles howled in a chorus of misery and hunger. In the shadows of a narrow pen, an old gnu, thin and bald, munched on the fibrous stems of manioc, now the mainstay of his meager diet.

Their grooming over, the boy poked the chimp in the ribs and the two began wrestling in the dust. Sure enough, when Patrice tried to pull away, the ape grabbed his shirt and it tore, and the play came to a sudden stop.

The chimpanzee crawled back to the iron stake and sat. One hand supported the iron collar as he watched the boy walk away.

The nun hid in the shadows of the labor room as he dropped back into the hospital grounds. With a little smile, he padded back to his pavilion, the torn shirt evidence of his night visit.

The Congolese sister looked at both of us. "That is really what happened."

The reverend mother smiled at her. "Thank you for your good work. Now you had better get some rest." The young nun left, closing the door behind her.

"*Voilà*," said the superior, "there you are. As you will learn when you have been here for a while, it is difficult to teach discipline to the Africans. One never knows what they will do next."

"Come on, *ma mère*," I said. "He has no family. Let him keep his friend."

The reverend mother thought for a moment. "You are right, *Docteur,* these are extraordinary and unhappy times." She stood up and walked me to the door. "Anyway, he doesn't really need a shirt until the weather turns cold."

CHAPTER 18

Le Patron

D URING THE COLD WAR the leader of a "client state" was
useful to the West if he could be kept faithful to our
ideas of freedom and democracy with inducements of
arms and money. So long as he voted for Western
positions in the UN and welcomed Western personnel and
equipment into his country, the leader, whether dictator
or patron of an oligarchy, was wined and dined in Western
capitals. Entrepreneurs out for the "quick buck" swarmed
into the client state and, if wealthy enough to sweeten
deals with gratuities, became part of the privileged
national elite.

Let me hasten to add that I have few academic
qualifications to make such broad statements. I am
neither an historical scholar nor a political scientist. I am
simply a physician with a physician's point of view, often
myopic and focused on an individual and his family.
Someday a full, updated biography of President Mobutu
will be written. To be accurate, such a work must wait
until time and history have played out their hands long
enough to allow for perspective and fact to replace bias
and myth.

As his physician, I was witness to the fact that
Mobutu's career spanned a time when the nations of
Central Africa became independent from previous
colonial masters. In the Congo, which became Zaire in
1971, economic and cultural bonds remained and were
exploited in a variety of imaginative ways. Mobutu's
prolonged stay in power allowed him to be a key player
(or nonplayer, depending on your point of view) in the

131

transition from dictatorship to democracy.

Men far wiser than I will have to differentiate between traditional African democracy and traditional Western democracy. These sages will also define how various forms of so-called democracy function today both in Africa and the West. They will specify the roles played by money and weapons in the formulation of what passes for government by the people. If an informed, intelligent, freely cast vote is the sine qua non of democracy, we are on perilous ground in America and have a long way to go in Africa. In the United States, a hopeful politician, brimming with enthusiasm and a sense of duty to his fellowman, is more likely to be asked by his party, "How much money can you raise for your campaign?" before "What do you stand for?" After all, image makers, pollsters, and others interposed between the voters and their representative are expensive (not unlike the "bureaucrats" that infect the medical profession). After reality has rubbed the fuzz off his high intentions, the politician is indeed bought by those who paid for him to run. The voice of the people is stifled by money—big money of vested interests with powerful lobbies. So it was in Africa.

Unthinkable questions have been raised by controversial African leaders like Arap Moi of Kenya, the Tutsi rebels of Rwanda, the Zulus of South Africa, to name a few. "Is the West's idea of democracy necessarily the wisest route to representative government in Africa?"

General Mobutu became president following his second bloodless coup d'état in 1965. To me, as well as to most of the Congolese people, he became *Le Patron—* The Boss.

What motivated Mobutu to take over the government for a second time in 1965? Who were his backers? What role did he play as president of a "client state" during the cold war? Time will tell. This chapter answers a different question: "What was it like to be his personal physician?"

For the better part of fourteen years I addressed Mobutu as *mon général* or *patron*. Only later was he addressed as *Maréchal*. I spent months at a time traveling all over the country and all over the world with him. In those days his goal was to unite the 250 tribes scattered throughout a territory a third the size of the United States. To a great measure, he succeeded.

My relationship with Mobutu had a profound effect on me as a physician. I was also, on occasion, an observer of great-power realpolitik practiced with all the tra-la-la and camouflage that have come to characterize modern diplomacy. Old-fashioned statesmanship was, and still is, at a premium.

A few weeks after independence Dr. Pirquin and I were operating around the clock in Léopoldville on wounded soldiers, police, and civilians caught up in the political and tribal fighting. Like all doctors, I thought of prophylaxis and wondered whether Mobutu, then a colonel army chief of staff, might be able to prevent some of the conflicts and ease our load in the operating room. With this in mind, I stationed myself outside the gate to his home in the paratrooper camp and flagged him down as he drove out.

He rolled down the window. "*Oui?*" he asked, clearly surprised to see a solitary white man in the camp.

"I'm a surgeon at the *Hôpital des Congolais,* and I wondered if you could do something about the violence in town so we can catch up at the hospital."

He looked even more surprised at my directness and, maybe, naïveté but replied, "Yes, I think I can," and drove off.

To this day, I don't know what he did, but not long after that the influx of trauma into the hospital seemed to decrease.

Shortly after this I was called to his home to remove the fish bone from his great-aunt's throat, then to sit with the dying aunt and family. My next call was to circumcise his newborn son. Although I had been subjected to some of the best training in surgery available in the United States, I had neither seen nor performed a circumcision. I scurried around to find some very small "mosquito" clamps and fine sutures. A Gomko clamp, a sort of semiautomatic circumciser, was nowhere to be found. I learned from Sam and Eugene in the operating room that a circumcision must be done with proper guarantees that the victim's penis remain unblemished and completely functional. The removal of too little foreskin would be as unacceptable as removing too much. Above all, postcircumcision bleeding was considered the mark of a novice and a complication to be avoided at all cost.

After quieting the infant with a ball of powdered sugar wrapped in gauze and soaked in cognac, I went to work and tied off every tiny bleeder I could see and probably some that never existed. The cut ends of sutures and ties bristled around the tip of his tiny penis, making it look like a newborn porcupine. I stayed long enough to ensure that not a drop of blood would be lost and that the little boy could pee with the gusto of Brussels' famous statue. The colonel was impressed, and I was greatly relieved.

Following this, I was frequently called to "doctor" the colonel's family. When he became a general and commander in chief of the Congolese Army, I left the hospital to become chief doctor for the army. On November 25, 1965, the general became president. A couple of months later he asked me to be his personal physician. The framed certificate hangs above my desk in Wyoming. It states:

DEMOCRATIC REPUBLIC OF THE CONGO
OFFICE OF THE CHIEF OF STATE
CERTIFICATE

WE, LIEUTENANT-GENERAL JOSEPH-DÉSIRÉ MOBUTU, PRESIDENT OF THE REPUBLIC, CERTIFY BY THIS DOCUMENT THAT MR. CLOSE WILLIAM, DOCTOR IN MEDICINE, IS ATTACHED TO THE PRESIDENCY AS A MEDICAL ADVISOR.

HE IS AUTHORIZED, AS NEEDED, TO DON THE UNIFORM OF THE NATIONAL CONGOLESE ARMY AND TO WEAR A LIEUTENANT-COLONEL'S INSIGNIA.

LÉOPOLDVILLE, 19 FEBRUARY 1966.

THE PRESIDENT OF THE REPUBLIC
SIGNED: MOBUTU J.D.
LIEUTENANT-GENERAL

His signature was a jog with a tail and two sweeping strokes of his green pen that crossed the page.

The first time I actually saw Mobutu in action was in response to a call I received from a good friend John Sinclair, the British military attaché and a colonel in the Black Watch.

"Doctor, there's a mutiny at the police barracks. The general is on his way there. I'll pick you up."

We arrived at the police camp in the middle of town as the general was walking through the front gates. Several hundred gray-uniformed men stood resolutely in a semicircle fifty yards away, pointing their rifles at him. Most of them seemed tired and surly; a few in the front row looked defiant. John and I, and three of the paratroopers who had been in the general's Jeep, started through the gates behind him. He glanced over his shoulder.

"Where are you going? Go back," he ordered. We did, and watched from the gates.

Mobutu halted some twenty yards in front of the police. Slowly and deliberately he scrutinized the men. Then, standing at attention with his shoulders back and fists clenched, he commanded, "*Déposez vos armes*—Drop your weapons." A low murmur came from the men, then silence. No one moved. The only sound was the dull roar of city traffic in the background. The men glanced at each other, their rifles leveled at the general. I held my breath. Two men in the front row dropped the butts of their rifles, released their grip on the barrels, and the guns clattered to the ground. Another rifle fell, and in seconds, the crashing of weapons echoed in the camp. A handful of men in the front row stepped forward and saluted.

When I took over the Congolese Army Medical Corps I was given an empty office in the headquarters building. I knew nothing about military medicine, and when Mobutu asked me to set up a field hospital in the eastern part of the country where fighting between central government troops and rebel units was continuing, I had to admit that I had no experience in this sort of thing. His response was, "Just apply Article Fifteen."

I walked downstairs to the office of an experienced, senior Belgian officer and asked him rather diffidently, hating to display my ignorance, "The general told me to apply Article Fifteen in setting up a field hospital in the east. Would you mind telling me what that means?"

The officer roared with laughter. "Article Fifteen means *débrouillez-vous*—work it out any way you can."

As it turned out, a field hospital was not needed. I took on the next assignment: to deal with a renegade battalion camped on the outskirts of Baudouinville on Lake Tanganyika.

The eastern part of the Congo was relatively calm now. The renegade battalion had been chased out of Stanleyville by Belgian troops parachuted into the town to rescue white hostages. They made their way south, leaving a trail of smoking villages and corpses.

Some of the men had been involved in the massacre of Italian airmen and the ritual cannibalism that had followed the killings. This had frightened away many of the expatriates in the area and embarrassed Mobutu. Like many isolated army units in the interior, it had received no supplies or inspections for many months. Communications were nonexistent. My job was to "inspect" the unit and do what I could to bring them under the control of headquarters in the capital.

I took off from Luluabourg in the twin-engine Aztec and climbed rapidly through the overcast. Two and a half hours and I should be within sight of the huge lake. Since no radio navigational aids were functioning reliably in the country, I would have to let down through the overcast in two hours to pick up the Lualaba River, then follow it to the lake. I had learned to fly the rivers and had been lost enough times to develop a search-and-find-myself technique. The problem was that crossing a river didn't tell you whether you were north or south from your plotted course. I used a coin toss to choose and was lucky enough to have been right most of the time.

I turned on the autopilot, stretched my legs around the rudder pedals, and settled into the seat for the flight. I had synchronized the props, but the sound of the engines still undulated slowly, recurrent, soporific, and symphonic as higher-pitched tones crept into the harmony of the engines. With half-closed eyed, I scanned the instruments. In the air corps, we had been taught to fly the plane, leaving the navigation to the navigator and the engines to the crew chief. My ignorance kept me alert.

After two hours I started a gentle descent. Going down through an overcast when the ceiling was unknown wasn't something I liked to do, but the central part of the country was quite flat, and the risks not extreme. I broke out at four thousand feet. The visibility was to the horizons. The Lualaba River lay ahead, running north and south. To the north, I could see Kabalo, where the Italians had been killed. To the south, the Luvua formed the eastern fork of a Y flowing into Lake Moero while the Lualaba continued south to the copper country. I was relieved. It's a nice feeling to know where you are in such a situation.

Lake Tanganyika appeared on the horizon, and after flying over the lakeshore, I turned south, looking for the large Catholic mission near Baudouinville. I buzzed the church and circled the area. There seemed to be a military encampment not far from a dirt landing strip; otherwise the place looked deserted. A breeze off the lake bent the tall grasses next to the runway. I landed to the east and taxied back to the west end of the field to be in position for takeoff. I planned to make this mission as short as possible.

As I gunned the right engine to wheel the Aztec around, a large body of armed soldiers rose out of the grasses and surrounded the plane. A rush of fear squeezed my belly. I pushed my black bag out onto the wing and followed it, leading with my shoulders so the men could see the red crosses Tine had sewed on the night before. "*Monganga, monganga*—Doctor, doctor," I repeated, smiling and waving. They seemed to relax a little. They needed a doctor. They looked ragged and miserable.

With no supplies for months, these troops had terrorized people in the area and lived off their meager crops of corn, manioc, and papayas. The local women provided their only recreation, and as in many army units, gonorrhea was the major medical problem. To the Congolese, *la bleno,* as it was called, was a serious disease, not because it caused burning and frequent urination, but because, after a while, it affected their ability to have children. And a man without kids was not a man. Most soldiers were eager to do anything to cure the disease except curtail their exposure to it.

I walked to the camp with a lieutenant. The men who had been at the airstrip followed in a disorderly group, chattering among themselves. I told the officer that I had been sent by General Mobutu to bring them medicine and see how they were doing. The lieutenant, who was young and seemed well educated, apologized for my reception. He explained that the red markings on my aircraft made them think it was a Katangese plane, like the Fouga-Magister that had strafed them on their trek south. He ordered a soldier to run ahead and tell the commanding officer that a doctor had arrived. The man glared at me and started to object, but the officer waved him away and he set off at a lope toward a collection of tents and shacks.

After a few minutes we came to a large hut guarded by a corporal armed with an FAL semiautomatic rifle. I noticed with relief that there was no magazine clipped into the weapon. The lieutenant brushed past the guard. As I entered he was standing at attention saluting an officer who sat behind a rough wooden table. The officer, a captain, got up and, reaching across the table, shook my hand. He was a heavy man with a scar on his temple extending to the outer corner of his right eye and a long drooping mustache. His features were more finely chiseled and his skin lighter than most Congolese.

"Sit down, Doctor," he said. I sat on a stool the lieutenant put behind me and noticed a young woman squatting in a corner behind the captain. Her hair was braided into sharp spikes projecting from her scalp. She stared at me with large brown eyes; the whites were like young ivory. Her naked arms and shoulders were strong and shapely. Copper bracelets clinked softly as she raised her hand to cover her mouth and nose in the presence of a stranger.

"The general sent me to inspect your battalion and do what I can for your men," I said.

"You are the first person from headquarters we have seen in a long time. We have not been supplied for over a year."

"I will report what you have said to the general. I have brought some antibiotics to treat any infections in your men, including *la bleno*. If they will line up I can check them quickly and do what is necessary." The captain gave the order, the lieutenant saluted, then left.

"I doubt whether I have any disease, *Docteur,* but with these women you never know," said the captain. "Give me a shot of penicillin. And give one to her." I was happy to oblige.

As air corps cadets during the war we were subjected to weekly "short arm" parades. We stepped up and unzipped in front of a medical officer seated on a stool. After obeying the order to "skin it back and milk it down," those who showed evidence of a venereal disease were sent to an office for treatment. Those who passed the test zipped up and walked out, happy and relieved. I gave "peter parade" instructions to the lieutenant and took my place at the head of the line.

As the men marched past I divided them into three groups. The largest was made up of those infected, as evidenced by a drop of pus clinging to the end of their penis. The second very small group consisted of a handful of men without the disease. Into the third group I gathered those who were clearly arrogant renegades—all of whom had gonorrhea. I told these "special cases" that their disease was serious enough to warrant special care. The other, less critical "positives" would be given penicillin injections by the battalion medical aide after I left.

After turning over supplies of syringes and penicillin, I quickly boarded the plane, and bounced down the strip and into the air for Albertville, an hour to the north on the lakeshore, where I made arrangements for a military plane to pick up the renegade troops that had been chosen for "special" treatment.

In 1968, the president asked me to take over the fifteen-hundred bed general hospital in Kinshasa. With the help of doctors recruited from the United States, Canada, and Europe, I renovated and staffed the hospital, turning it into a national referral center of over two thousand beds. Our occupancy rates often reached 120 percent. The hospital—renamed Mama Yemo after the president's mother—became in the 1980s one of the biggest centers in Africa for patients with AIDS. Also, because of widespread malnutrition among children in the city, we created health centers in the slums where we taught mothers how to prepare a high-protein gruel from soya seed, small fish, and grubs, which were readily available and cheap.

The president took a great deal of interest in the general hospital. Occasionally I took him on early-morning rounds, introducing him to individual patients and explaining our efforts to deal with their problems. As far as I was concerned, he was at his best at these times and I had glimpses of what a wonderful father of the nation he could be if he were ever separated from the day-to-day political melee.

I traveled with him frequently on his large riverboat up the Congo. When we stopped at a village, patients lined up to come aboard, where I examined them and did what I could for them medically. The president often watched and encouraged a mother with a newborn or an old man hobbling up the gangway on swollen feet with running sores caused by parasites. These "onboard" dispensaries were unhurried, and although I know we saw only a tiny handful of people, something positive occurred for the patients and certainly for me and the president.

We often stopped at Bolobo, a British Baptist mission hospital, run by Dr. Bernard McCullough and his Scandinavian wife. One of the president's children was born there during an earlier trip, and Mobutu had a special place in his heart for both the mission and the McCulloughs.

Once, on a night trip upriver, the president and I leaned on the wooden railing to watch the shoreline illuminated by a searchlight on the bridge. As if crowded by the forest behind, giant trees bent over the water and small groups of people on strips of sand flashed by in the beam of light. Moments later, after darkness had reclaimed the people, their shouts, "*Oyé, Mobutu . . . Oyé, Mobutu*," reached us across the water.

"There is your voice of the people," said the president with a dry laugh. "It's *Oyé, Mobutu* when beer and bread are cheap. If the prices rise, they will shout *Abat Mobutu* and shake their fists at me."

The president loved the river and the river people. His boat became one of the rare places where he had time to read and reflect. Out of our talks on some of the trips came the concept of a floating hospital.

The hospital riverboat was a seven-hundred-ton unit my son, Sandy, and I designed. It was designed with the idea of working small segments of the Congo River and to update public health and training as well as take care of acute needs. The vessel was baptized *Marie Antoinette,* after the president's first wife. The crew and medical staff were all Zairian.

The floating hospital was such a showpiece, with two operating rooms, screening clinics, X ray and lab, wards, etc., that the president insisted that every time it left Kinshasa it must go all the way to Kisangani (ex-Stanleyville), a trip of over two thousand kilometers. Two smaller boats, hoisted on davits on the afterdeck below the helicopter pad, were used to do advanced screening so that when the hospital boat arrived, we could take patients on board and do what surgery was needed. This was not the ideal use of the boat, since there was too little time to retrain the village medical personnel and attend to more general public health needs. The log of one such trip reads as follows:

> *May 3, 1971: The* Marie Antoinette *returns. She left Kinshasa April 13, returned May 2. She visited 109 villages. The doctors did 77 operations and saw 5,134 patients. They had 17 workdays. There were 15 serious hospitalizations, two deaths, and one birth.*

The president was very pleased with the boat's activities, but unfortunately this beautiful "showcase unit" taught me a difficult lesson: it proved to be far too expensive to operate. After several years of service it was lashed to an old dock and abandoned to gather rust.

Mobutu was thoughtful and generous with my family. He and *Madame* came to a small dinner party in our home at the paratrooper camp when Tine and I celebrated our twenty-fifth wedding anniversary. The Belgian caterer who had been in the Congo most of his life was sure that the president would not show up. After all, he was much too busy and, he implied, much too important. When Mobutu did show up, promptly at the time set for dinner, the caterer was profuse in his welcome.

On one occasion, twenty-four hours after returning from a trip to Europe, the president had to leave on another official trip. The usual departure ceremonies were under way. His motorcade stopped next to the reviewing stand set up in front of the VIP lounge at the airport. The crew of his DC-10 waited along the red carpet at the foot of the forward stairs, and the diplomatic corps and members of his government stood in line behind the reviewing stand. The president stepped out of his limo and waved to the people watching from the apron in front of the terminal. Tine and the kids, Sandy and Tina, were standing next to me in the crowd. We were catching a few more moments together. The president climbed the three steps of the reviewing stand, saluted the colors, and the military band played the national anthem. As he started down the diplomatic line I kissed Tine and the kids good-bye and joined others walking out to the aircraft. The president would be the last one on board. As I started up the steps I turned and saw that the president had left the diplomatic line and was walking toward the VIP lounge. Tine and the kids had detached themselves from the crowd and were coming to meet him. They stood together for a moment, shook hands, then the president turned and walked to the plane. Tine and the kids stayed where they were and waved. I waved back.

Tine told me later that Mobutu had called out, "*Madame, Madame,*" while pointing toward her. She looked around to see which *Madame* he was calling. A security man ran up and told her that the president wanted to see her and the children. Surprised, and a little embarrassed at being picked out of the crowd, they followed the security man.

The president greeted them. "*Bonjour, Madame, et les enfants.*" They all shook hands. "I am sorry to take the doctor away from you so soon after our return yesterday, but I need him. I hope you understand."

"*Oui, Général,*" Tine replied. "*Et bon voyage.*" She said the general had given her and the kids one of his big, warm smiles. Sandy, our son, had tears in his eyes.

One of my major responsibilities was to travel with Mobutu both in the interior of the country and in the many overseas trips he undertook. At first, traveling in the presidential retinue had its thrills, but the novelty of riding in a limo behind the president, attending innumerable never-ending parades and state banquets with their usual tired pomp and cold food, wore off quickly. One becomes entrapped by protocol and the need to be available at any moment. A wise old man who trained U.S. secret-service personnel came to Zaire to supervise the training of the president's security detail. He told me always to remember that only a third of assassination attempts on heads of state would have been successful had the president's physician been within two meters of the target. This took some of the joy out of the assignment.

One long stretch of travels abroad in 1970 started with an annual trip to Switzerland, where Professor Alfredo Vannotti, who had become my mentor, reviewed the president's medical situation and gave his blessing to the care that I was giving him.

Starting in the midsixties, I accompanied the president to Switzerland for a checkup with the professor. At first we met at the Nestlé Clinic in Lausanne, where Dr. Vannotti was the chief of medicine. Then, when he retired from the university, Mobutu and I traveled to the Clinique Valmont. Over the years Vannotti and I became friends as well as colleagues. The visits were a source of stimulation and wisdom for me. Vannotti had been physician to heads of state and rulers of business empires from all over the world. He was a much-respected scientist, a wise clinician, and was armed with a healthy cynicism about human nature.

It is important, if you are the physician of a head of state, to have a world-recognized authority involved in your patient's care. Once, I received a terse letter from an officer in the president's security team stating that if anything happened to "*Le Guide*" I would be dealt with summarily.

On this particular visit, Vannotti had found the president in excellent shape, but suggested more relaxation, a healthy diet, and more exercise. This was a prescription for health that I needed as well.

The president took Vannotti's advice to heart and, the next day, invited by his friend and ally King Hassan, we left for a seven-day private visit to Morocco. Every morning we were up early to work out in the hotel gym. Afterward, the president had a massage, then I joined him to parboil in a hammam, the Arab version of a steam bath. The morning ended with a swim in the pool. We competed to see who could swim underwater the farthest. He could. Afternoons we went on excursions into the mountains. We visited the citadel at Meknes, roaming through the immense grain storage vaults built by Christian slaves in the Middle Ages. One evening we were guests of the king at his palace in Meknes, and dined under a starlit sky in a courtyard surrounded by filigreed archways. We visited the souk at Marrakesh, bought rugs and leather footrests, and saw the terrace at the *Hôtel des Anglais,* where Churchill played backgammon during the war.

Another evening we were invited to the home of a Moroccan woman noted for her cooking. We sat on thick carpet. A mountain of finely spiced couscous with almonds was brought in, and we served ourselves with our left hands. Mishoui—a whole roast lamb on a spit—was carried in by two men and set on a rack so we could choose which part of the meat we preferred. Our hostess tried to ply the president with food, but he stuck to a Vannotti-imposed diet and, in a diplomatic move, apologized to her for his doctor's poor showing at her table. Her attention immediately switched from him to me, and although I was already stuffed to the ears, she piled more food onto my plate. After the meal I needed help getting up.

From there we had gone to a small nightclub, and around midnight, the president bet Morocco's chief of protocol that his doctor could beat the king's military aide at tennis the next day. The king's aide was a colonel in the Moroccan Paratroopers and looked to be in much better condition than I was, but I had no say in the bet or the challenge.

The next morning, at high noon, the colonel and I met on the center court at the Hilton. I had hurried into town to buy a pair of white shorts and tennis shoes. It was very hot, and I was still recovering from the meal of the night before. As we started to warm up, the minister of youth and tourism appeared with a TV crew and a silver cup. The colonel was a short stocky man who jumped around the court with ferocious intensity. Happily, his strength was not matched by his accuracy, and his shots were out more often than not. I remembered a few tips from a little book called *How to Win Without Actually Cheating*, and as the colonel became more and more upset, I remained calm. I won, and still have the silver cup. Afterward I went to my room, took a shower, and slept. I dreamed of

Arabian palaces, dancing slaves, and the Atlas Mountains made of couscous and almonds.

Every visiting head of state lays a wreath at the Tomb of the Unknown Soldier in Arlington. Tine and I were part of Mobutu's party in 1970 when he was on an official visit to Washington and the United States. Tine and I stayed at Blair House, and attended the White House banquet with the president. The historical setting of Arlington Cemetery, our national anthem, the flags snapping in the breeze under a bright blue sky, and the precision drill of the honor guard brought memories of ceremonies when I was a cadet officer in the air corps and made me proud to be American, showing *Le Patron* one of our most sacred monuments to those who gave their lives for freedom.

After Washington, President Mobutu and his whole party flew out to Los Angeles for a special tour of Disneyland. Our oldest daughter was living in Oakland. She joined us with her small daughter, Shona. We all boarded the pirate ship. As we sailed slowly and majestically past a Wild West fort, rifles poked through loopholes in the logs and the president's security men reached for their weapons. I shouted, *"Non, non, c'est du Mickey Mouse,"* in time to avoid a counterattack. It was a happy time with the president and some of the family.

Most evenings I called on the president at his home in the paratrooper camp. He liked to play checkers. He played very fast, and I rarely won even when I caught him cheating, which he frequently did. Sometimes, to tease me, he played a recording of de Gaulle's speech attacking American policy in Vietnam. I had mixed feelings about Vietnam, but my feelings about de Gaulle were decidedly negative. He thoroughly enjoyed his victories and my losses, especially when my patience wore thin.

One evening, after I won two of the thirteen games I had set as a maximum number I would play in one

My dad, Edward B. Close, Sr.,
Managing Governor of the American
Hospital of Paris

Bill and Bettine, secretly engaged at 16

Bettine and Bill, married 1943 in Greenwich, Connecticut

Family photo in Greenwich, Connecticut, home, 1953.
(l to r) Tina, Tine, Jessie, Sandy, Bill, Glennie.
(Horses: Nubbins, Stargrain, Brownie; dogs: Ben and Taffy)

Bill, U.S. Army Air Corps Cadet

Bill, Troop Carrier Pilot—St. Andrè de l'Eure, Normandy, France

Moral Re-Armament showing of film *Freedom*, in the Kasai, pre-independence

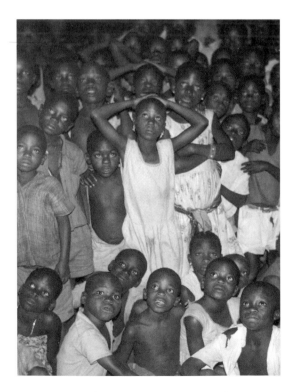

Congolese crowd watching *Freedom*

Downtown Léopoldville (Kinshasa) in early 1960s

Two thousand-bed Mama Yemo General Hospital in early 1970s

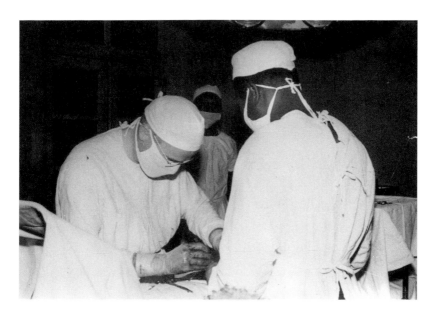

Dr. Bill Close operating with Eugene and Samuel,
Léopoldville General Hospital in early 1960s

Registering three hundred fifty operations per month

Dr. Bill Close and *La Mère de la Pharmacie* receiving
gifts of medical supplies

Crossing the Lualaba River during a meningitis epidemic

Patrice's friend, the chimp

President Mobutu waving at the crowd next to Dr. Bazunga,
Hospital Director, and Dr. Bill Close

Dr. Bill Close and Deanne Bradley, R.N.

Chuck

Tine and Bill at home in Big Piney with dogs,
(l to r) Katie, Baggie, Angie, and Freedog

Dr. Bill Close

Bill fly-fishing on the Green River, Big Piney, Wyoming

evening, he offered me a cognac. As we moved out onto the terrace he laughed and proclaimed, "As Napoleon used to say, '*J'ai failli perdre*—I almost lost.' "

People have often asked me what it was like to be so close to the president. I've always answered that being a physician and friend to a chief of state is an enormous responsibility. With Mobutu, this responsibility was made easier by his almost constant good humor and courtesy. I was never subjected to unreasonable demands or the arrogance that is sometimes associated with power, which, I have been told by other presidential physicians, is not unusual behavior for a head of state.

I have also been asked if I was ever frightened—really scared. The answer is yes, of course.

Once, when I was about to leave Tine and the children in Switzerland to return to Africa, I was overcome with the feeling that I would never see them again. I bought each a painted carving of a saint but did not tell them what fear lay behind the gifts.

Flying my own plane was frequently scary. Once, after a two A.M. takeoff, I flew into a thunderstorm and thought I was in a submarine being depth-bombed from above. I broke out into full moonlight over the endless forest. I chilled as the sweat dried on my shirt and my mouth was pasty with fear. I was lost. A ribbon of water glinted below; I tossed a mental coin, turned south, and with my guardian angel heaving a sigh of relief, I recognized the landmarks below and flew on.

In the summer of 1968, I was scared when we landed at the military airport outside Brussels for a secret meeting between Mobutu and King Baudouin arranged by Prince d'Arenberg and, to a lesser degree, by me. There were reports that our cars would be targets of ex-mercenaries angered by the president. Our two cars were surrounded by motorcycle police and we raced, at breakneck speed, into town on back roads until we wheeled under the portals of the palace in the center of town.

On another occasion I was frightened when the lights went out all over the paratrooper camp. Feeling trapped by my responsibility, I jumped in my car and raced to the president's house. A guard at the front gate flashed a light on my face and, recognizing me, snapped to attention—*"mon colonel."* Other troopers pushed open black iron gates. Searchlights from Brazzaville, across the river, swept the presidential compound and the riverbank next to the road at the end of the gardens. The lights left fleeting images of murky water with bobbing clumps of hyacinth and of the marble terrace and white facade of the building. I drove past the house and swung around to park next to the front door. My headlights flashed across three security men in full combat outfits.

Walking into the front hall I asked, *"Ça va?"*

"Ça va," replied the senior man, handing me a flashlight.

I went upstairs to the president's room. The door was open. It was pitch-black inside, and I didn't see him until the sweeping beam of a searchlight backlit his tall form at the window.

"Bonsoir, mon général," I said, stepping into the room.

"Bonsoir, Docteur," he replied, without turning.

I sat on the bed; he remained at the window. We waited . . . waited for the lights to come back on, or for an attack. Rumors of assassination plots were rife. Those leading the bloody rebellion that was sweeping across the country, as well as their Cuban and Chinese allies, were across the river in Brazzaville. The feel of the snub-nosed .36 in my pocket gave me little comfort.

After what seemed like a long time, the lights flickered on and off, and finally stayed on.

"*Merci, Docteur*," said the president, turning away from the window.

"*Bonne nuit, mon général*," I replied, and went back to my house in the camp.

CHAPTER 19

Leaving Africa

DESPITE THE FEARS and frustrations, leaving Zaire was tough. I had been there since independence in 1960, through the mutiny, the Katanga secession, and the savage, bloody civil war between the central government backed by the West and the insurgents backed by Cuba and China. Two-thirds of the country was overrun by rebel "Simbas" who massacred all those who could read and write.

The reorganization and expansion of Mama Yemo Hospital had been a great challenge. I hated to leave my friends on the staff, especially since what we created together would probably collapse from lack of funds. For years I saw the president daily. He supported our efforts to establish an honest, efficient medical organization. During my last couple of weeks in Kinshasa, however, some of the rats had started to come out of the woodwork: Zairians and expatriates were maneuvering for positions of control in the hospital so they could fire rivals in the never-ending struggle for power and money. I was sure that things would get worse. Government funds for health care and social services had almost dried up.

I walked over to the president's office and found him reading reports out on the grass terrace off the living room. His favorite place to work was at a white metal garden table shaded by a striped umbrella. From his chair he had an unobstructed view of the Kinsuka Rapids, where the Congo River narrowed after the pool and started its race to the coast. Distance muted the roar of the cataracts. Closer at hand, the cries of peacocks and parrots in the presidential zoo mixed with the music of a Zairian band coming from a radio set on the table.

"Good morning, *Docteur*. You have a problem?" asked the president.

"Yes, *mon général*. We need more zaires to feed the patients at Mama Yemo, especially the children. We budgeted for enough, but prices have gone way up."

"I cannot authorize any out-of-budget expenses," he replied.

"I know that, *patron*, but I have an idea. Independence Day comes next week. Air Force jets will fly over the grandstands as they have in the past. Why not cancel that, and give me the money for jet fuel to buy food?"

"That is impossible. Of course, the jets will fly in a salute to the country."

"But what about the money to feed the patients?"

"You don't know anything about politics. The government has to show its strength. *Comment va Madame?*" he asked, turning back to his reading. The president always asked about my wife when he wanted to change the subject.

The blood rose to my head. "*Madame* is fine, *mon général*. But if your people could hope that the situation for them and their children might improve, that would be good politics for the government," I said, raising my voice.

He replied angrily, "You cannot speak to the chief of state that way."

"I'm sorry to have raised my voice," I said more quietly, "but what can I do to feed the patients in the hospital named Mama Yemo after your mother?"

He looked out over the rapids for a moment. "How much do you need?"

I told him.

He picked up the telephone and called the governor of

the national bank. "*Le Docteur* Close will come to your office. Give him the zaires he needs to buy food for the hospital." He hung up and went back to his reading.

"*Merci, patron,*" I said, and left.

The chief of protocol and the head of security had heard the exchange from the living room. "Everything all right?" they inquired as I brushed by them.

"Just fine," I said. "*Pas de problem*—No problem."

I would miss the president. We'd been through a lot together. He had said to me many times, "*En tout cas, on a beaucoup souffert ensemble*—After all is said and done, we have suffered through much together." At the end of a very hard day, he would say, "*Quel pays*—What a country! How would you like to run a country like this?" I always answered, "I wouldn't. It's tough enough being your doctor."

At the end of June in 1976, I landed in Geneva after an eight-hour flight from Kinshasa. As the other passengers headed for the terminal I went to the rear of the plane and waited for my old black lab, Trooper. Two baggage handlers came out of the hold carrying his cage and set it on the ramp. When Trooper saw me, he barked and his tail strummed on the bars. I let him out, and he looked up at me and smiled with his gray muzzle as he emptied his bladder against a lamppost. His gums were bleeding from efforts to chew his way through the bars. I was relieved to get him out of Zaire. Next to my wife and kids, he was my best friend.

We headed for baggage and customs. The other passengers had long since reached the terminal. Suddenly Trooper put on the brakes and deposited a sizable mound on the Swiss-clean floor. Nobody was around. The only paper I had was *Time* magazine. I covered the mess with it. Carter, Reagan, and Ford were on the cover. I meant no disrespect. At customs, I said to the inspector, "I'm terribly sorry, but my old dog pooped in the hall. We have just come in on an eight-hour flight from Africa."

"Never mind," he replied. "The Italians will clean it up."

He chalked my suitcase, we headed to a car rental desk, and finally were on our way to Valmont in a little Renault. There was no rush. My friend Vannotti didn't expect us until after lunch. It was a beautiful autumn day. The Swiss countryside, neat and unlittered, helped to restore order in my cluttered mind. Scarlet geraniums and variegated petunias in a riot of color grew in farmhouse window boxes and in huge pots hanging from roof beams. The lake shimmered in the distance, and the French side was ill-defined in the morning haze.

I was hungry. The food on Air Zaire had been awful— leathery cold cuts and a chicken *mwambe* swimming in cold grease and palm oil. There had been plenty of warm beer pulled from a wooden crate dragged along the aisle by a sweating air hostess.

Just before Lausanne, I pulled off the main road, drove down to the lake, and stopped at a little restaurant with a terrace overlooking the water. It was early for lunch, and the place was empty. Trooper and I sat at a small table under the trellis. Dogs are allowed everywhere in Switzerland. The waiter came, neat and efficient, a folded napkin hung over his left forearm.

"*Bonjour, monsieur. Ah, quel bon vieux chien*—What a good old dog," he exclaimed. Trooper glanced at me, gave the waiter a smile, and lay down. I explained that we had just flown in from Africa and were very hungry. He gave me a menu and disappeared. A few minutes later he returned with a large red enamel dog bowl with LE CHIEN written on the side. It was filled with a succulent hash of raw meat and cooked vegetables. Trooper wolfed down the food, crawled under the table, and with a big contented sigh, went to sleep. I ordered Wiener schnitzel and a bottle of Swiss white wine.

Food in Kinshasa, and certainly at the presidency, had been a good, if heavy, Belgian cuisine. But in 1971, after the Congo was renamed Zaire and the statues of King Leopold II and Stanley had been removed from their places of honor to a dump outside the city, European food had been replaced, especially at the presidency, by authentic African dishes. *Authenticité* had become the order of the day. Goat, porcupine, huge river catfish, and monkey meat—called by the Zairians, but only by the Zairians, *cousin*—had replaced filet mignon.

After eating, I sat back and looked out across the lake to the distant peaks of the Dents du Midi. A gentle breeze off the water rustled the vine leaves on the trellis. The edge of the red-and-white-checkered tablecloth fluttered quietly. I ordered an espresso and a cognac. No need to rush now.

The last month had been frantic. I had to get away. I wanted to be with Tine and the kids at our ranch in Wyoming—our place to get off the world, our retreat, my escape. So many things whirling around in my head; so much that needed to be done that couldn't be done in Zaire. How could the small black bag I had carried to the Congo sixteen years ago have become such a monster?

I reached under the table, found the old dog's head, and softly scratched behind his ear. The lake was glassy smooth and the occasional light breezes ruffled patches of water as they came ashore. I tried to relax in the tranquillity of the place. I couldn't remember not being on call. I couldn't remember not being somewhere where people, who had a right to demand my time and attention, couldn't find me. Now, for once, no one knew where I was, and no radio was strapped to my hip to tell them. I had been on call for so many things. On call to the hospital and to my practice. On call to the president. On distant call to Tine and the kids. Too distant, probably.

The waiter came and I paid the bill, with a good tip.

Trooper woke up and stretched. "Come on, old dog, time to move on."

I drove through Vevey, along the lakeshore into Montreux, then up the small steep road to Glion, and the clinic at Valmont. This institution was, and still is, old world and prestigious. People with means went there to recover their health and, sometimes, their perspective and humor.

The building hung on the side of the mountain and had a view of the lake through the tops of giant pines. A small bridge connected the third floor to the access road. I parked the car, opened the windows so Trooper had plenty of air, and walked in. The elevator took me slowly and sedately down to the first floor and the concierge. I introduced myself.

"Ah yes, Doctor, the professor is waiting for you in his office." I walked down the hall, opened the outer soundproof door, and knocked on the inner door. "*Oui*," resounded from inside, and I went in. Vannotti came from behind his desk with his arms outstretched. "*Cher ami*," he said as we embraced. "Sit down. How are you?"

He was a small man with wisps of gray hair on a balding head—one that seemed a little too big for his body. His blue eyes, behind gold-rimmed bifocals perched on the end of his nose, were expressive and worked in harmony with his constantly moving hands. He was in his early seventies but had looked the same for the last ten years. A black stethoscope stuck out of a pocket in his immaculate white coat.

"I'm fine," I answered. "Maybe a little weary."

He smiled and acknowledged this with his hand. "Sit down, please. We will have a little talk now, then I will finish these charts, and we can go for a walk." He settled behind his desk, his back to French doors that opened onto a small terrace. I pulled up an antique chair. He folded his hands and waited for me to speak.

"I hated to leave, but I had to get away. It was impossible to keep the hospital going. Most of the children have kwashi, and I had to fight with the general even to get local funds to buy the simplest foods in the market."

"How is the president?" asked the professor.

"Tired. Annoyed that I'm leaving." I paused. "He sends you his regards."

Vannotti acknowledged the thought with his hand. "Did you bring your old dog?" he asked.

"He's sleeping in the car."

"Give me half an hour to finish my work, and we'll go for a stroll on the mountain."

I went back to the car, let Trooper out, and walked down the steps to the garden terrace. The day was clear and fresh. High up, a plume of cloud like a pennant on a mast marked the peak of the Roches de Ney. The lake was deep blue, and the smell of pinesap filled the air. What a difference, what a contrast to Africa! I sat on the bench, put my feet on the low granite wall, and looked through the trees to the sky. I thought of the last time I had seen Vannotti.

The president was on an unofficial visit to Tunis. His fatigue, to which he would never admit, and some other medical signs were worrying me. I finally traced Vannotti to Milan and he agreed to hop a plane to Tunis. I met him at the airport, and during the drive to the Hilton where the president was staying, I told him of my concerns.

As I parked the car he said, "You must call me Alfred, not always *Monsieur le Professeur.*"

I replied, a bit embarrassed, "I couldn't do that. I

wouldn't be comfortable calling you Alfred."

"It means much to me to follow the work you are doing in Africa. And remember that I have known you for a long time, even back when you were trying to change people and the world at Caux. You call me Alfred, or I do not come again when you call me."

"Well, if you insist, *Monsieur le*—I mean Alfred." We both laughed. He donned his Borcelino at a rakish angle and followed me to the elevators and up to the presidential suite.

The visit went well, and my concerns proved to be of no major account. Vannotti encouraged the president to get some rest and exercise, and afterward I drove him back to the airport.

A hand on my shoulder awoke me. I got up and stretched the stiffness out of my limbs; the old dog was doing the same.

"I fell asleep," I said to the professor. "What a peaceful place. So calm and quiet. Well-ordered. Why can't the Africans be so organized?"

"They are in their own way," he replied. "Let's drive up the mountain. We can walk and then have something to eat in the café."

We drove up the steep narrow road past Caux in Vannotti's Alfa Romeo. The flags of several countries flew in front of the entrance to the Moral Re-Armament Center. A fleeting memory of enforced guilt went through me. I never wanted to go back into the place and sit at a table with missionary mentors to have my soul bared and purified by others. We climbed up to Les Avants. Leaving the car next to the café, we set out along a small dirt road that followed the mountain's convolutions. For a while neither of us spoke. Trooper walked ahead, his big tail rotating with pleasure. Around the next corner we came to a bench overlooking the lake. We sat. I whistled for

Trooper to come back.

"You have done a good job in Africa," said Vannotti. "Now it is time to return to your country, and your own people and family. You say you wish the Africans were organized as we are in Switzerland. Much of our organization is a product of our climate and our genes. Much of it is a thick crust overlying our humanity. We are terribly civilized and controlled, but we have as many suicides and alcoholics as most civilized countries. Did you see many suicides in Africa?"

"No, very few," I replied. "Many people were killed during the rebellion. But that was war. Now children are dying for lack of decent food."

We were quiet for a while. Then I continued, "Violence is different in Africa. In New York City, the violence we saw in the emergency room was more calculated. It was expected. No one got very emotional about a 'floater,' a 'jumper,' or a murder. In Africa, when the police and army fought, or tribes clashed, and people were killed or wounded, crowds gathered outside the operating room crying and screaming in distress over the brutality. Civilized violence is calculated. Uncivilized violence is more emotional, more glandular."

Vannotti nodded his agreement. "I have two patients who want to kill each other, but not in the usual way, with guns or knives." His English had a musical lilt, and kill became "keel." He was from the Tessin, the Italian-speaking part of Switzerland.

"Each is the head of a giant holding company. If one died, the other could easily take over the dead man's assets. Although they are what you Americans would call high livers—good cigars from Cuba, and the best wines and cognacs—they are both well-educated, civilized gentlemen." He painted the picture with a flourish of his hand. "One has coronary artery disease and hypertension;

the other, bleeding ulcers. Their maneuvers against each other's companies are sure to increase blood pressure in one and gastric acid in the other. I do the best I can to treat them, but someday one will die first and the other will win. *Ç'est comme ça*," he said, raising his hands and eyebrows, and shrugging his shoulders in a salute to immutable fate.

He turned to me and, shaking his head with a smile, said, "Beel, you would go after them both. You would explain to each that he must not be so aggressive. You would fight to change their ways; no more cigars, no more wine, no cognac. You would try to impose on them a regimen no monk could follow. You would try and remake them into what they are not—what they never could be. You want to cure everybody. You can't—*ç'est la comédie humaine*. Sometimes very funny, often very sad, and all you can do is listen carefully, sympathize, and go home. Maybe that is enough." He paused and we looked out over the trees to the lake. Fight, impose, remake. He is so right, I thought to myself.

The breeze off the mountain ruffled my hair and set up little dust devils next to the bench. Trooper chased a squirrel up a tree, barking slowly and hoarsely like old dogs do. I felt lost and useless, like flotsam on a beach washed up after a storm at sea. I looked at Vannotti. He smiled and said, "As you used to say in Africa, *ça ira*—It will work out."

"I hope so," I said.

"Look," he went on, putting his hand on my shoulder. "You have done things *fantastique* during your years in Africa. It has been *la grande aventure*."

"None of it was planned. One thing just led to another," I retorted, feeling a little defensive.

"Of course, of course," he replied, laughing. "How could it be planned? Adventure is never planned. It is marching through the door of opportunity into the unknown, with enthusiasm. You endured the storms and built up something *extraordinaire* in an impossible place."

"Probably too *extraordinaire*," I replied. "I think a lot of what we built will fall apart. The costs are huge, the country is broke, and the profiteers were starting to move in before I left."

"*Et alors*—so what? That is politics . . . another form of *la comédie humaine*. Now you must go to your mountains in Wyoming; look back, and look forward, and write. Write so people feel what you have felt, and so people will see what you have seen. And be with your family."

I took a deep breath of that clear pine-scented air and felt my shoulders relax as I exhaled. I stood up and stretched my arms and body.

"Thanks," I said. "That's a good prescription. I'll do my best."

"And relax a little, then you will do better," he said, with a smile.

I spent the night in one of the clinic's rooms and the next morning, after saying good-bye to my old friend, Trooper and I drove back to Geneva for the flight home.

PART THREE

Big Piney, Wyoming

1976–PRESENT

Introduction to
Big Piney, Wyoming

WE BOUGHT A RANCH in Big Piney, Wyoming, in 1975 while on a short visit to see our daughter Tina and our grandchildren, who were spending the summer in Jackson Hole. Even at that time we felt we would need some place to get off the world for a while after we left Africa. We had been driven to the ranch the first time by a real-estate man from Jackson. Nothing he showed us had been isolated enough until we drove into the mountains west of Big Piney. The ranch was at nine thousand feet and bordered the Bridger National Forest. The wildflowers were out in profusion, and we caught sight of a cow moose and her calf bedded down in a little glade through which a small, spring-fed brook ran down a gully to Muddy Creek. A herd of antelope ran parallel to the car as we climbed into the foothills, and veered off to our right as we drove into an aspen woods. The owner, Gordon Mickelson, was the grandson of one of the first ranchers to come into the area. He and his wife, Margaret, brought a lunch up the mountain from their home in Big Piney. Our new acquaintances, who became good friends and wonderful neighbors over the next few years, made us feel we had come home. They invited us to spend the rest of our leave at the ranch.

The next day we drove down to the rodeo at the fairgrounds near Big Piney. We had never been to a small-town rodeo before. We sat on a bleacher next to the main gate into the arena, the stock chutes to the left, the pens and chutes for bucking horses and bulls to the right. Pickup trucks surrounded the ring with families sitting on the cabs or in the back on portable chairs. Everyone seemed to know each other, kids ran around, and young people rode their horses proudly. Riders and horses were handsomely turned out for the occasion.

After the water truck had finished dampening the soil in the arena, cowboys carrying the American flag and the flag of Wyoming anchored to their stirrup leathers galloped in, followed by the rodeo queen and her attendants. Then pairs of riders, each carrying one of the western state flags, split into two files galloping around the ring in opposite directions as fast as they could. The crowd cheered them on with yells and car horns. The riders met in the center, forming a line of state flags behind the Stars and Stripes and Wyoming flag.

The noise of the crowd died away. A horse stamped and shook his bridle. A child cried. A bull butted the bars of his chute. The smell of dust and horse manure, sage, and hot cars was in the air. The sun was high. A single trumpeter started the national anthem and everyone stood up. Men took off their hats and held them over their hearts. I felt overwhelmed with pride for my country. It was hard to keep away the tears. How long we had been away!

After the anthem the announcer read "The Cowboy's Prayer" by Badger Clark. I was struck by the lines "Just let me live my life as I've begun/ And get me work that's open to the sky/ Make me a partner of the wind and sun,/ And I won't ask a life that's soft and high." As the prayer ended car horns blared and everybody cheered as the flag bearers and rodeo royalty galloped out of the arena.

Rodeos are rodeos. Men get tossed in the air. Cowgirls race around barrels at impossible angles, their horses slavering as they respond to the bat in the final seconds.

Calves are roped, thrown to the ground, and tied. Flaggers wave with authority. Steers are wrestled into the dirt as shirts get torn, and hips are jammed into their sockets. No bulldogger ever keeps his hat on. People had fun. Kids were peeled off the railings to climb back up again. The young rode around the area between the pickups and the beer shack, the chutes and the sloppy-joe trailer.

Having had several beers, I retired to the outhouse. I went in where it said cowboys. It was a two-holer. As I started to find relief the door opened and a cowboy—he had on chaps and a hat—came in and stood in front of the other hole. He had also had several beers. He blew out his breath as his bladder started to empty. As relaxation settled in he turned to me and said, "Hi. You new here? Ain't seen ya around."

"I am new," I replied. "We just bought a little ranch up in the hills."

"Great," he said as he shook off the last drops, "gonna push cows?"

"No," I replied, trying to do up the tin buttons on my new jeans. "I'm a doctor."

"Jeez, you don't say," he said. Pulling up his zipper, he rushed out yelling, "Hey, you guys, we got us a doctor!" I was ushered to the beer shack and met new friends.

CHAPTER 20

Into the Rocky Mountains

AFTER THE SHORT VISIT with Vannotti in June 1976, we landed at Kennedy. Trooper was fine. His smile got us through customs in record time. We flew to Salt Lake City and chartered a small plane for the flight to Big Piney, Wyoming. Troop went to sleep on the back seat. Small planes were nothing new to him. He had flown copilot for me on many trips in Africa. He would sit in the right seat and look out the window at the clouds and the sky. If the air was particularly choppy, he might drool on the throttle quadrant, but he never actually got airsick.

Tine, Tina, and her kids were at the airport to meet us. What a happy day. We set out for the ranch, thirty-five miles up in the Wyoming range. Our road was a primitive track going through Meadow Canyon up a switchback onto Antelope Flats. It dipped into North Muddy Creek, wound up to Fear Flats, and passing next to groves of aspen and spruce, ended at the ranch—640 acres tucked into the mountains. A high mountain plateau led the hiker or the cowboy to Old Baldy, Bare Mountain, Schyler Mountain, and Triple Peak, to mention just a few. To the east, across the Green River Valley, rose the Wind River Range, jagged and snow-covered, ending beyond the horizon at South Pass.

Big Piney was, at that time, in the county with the smallest population, in the state with the smallest population in the United States. After sixteen years of a high-profile job in an anxiety-provoking area, we wanted a place where we could get off the world quietly and happily, read, maybe write, and certainly be with our dogs and old horse in relative tranquillity.

During the process of settling in, I went to the little clinic in Big Piney and told the nurse practitioner that I would be happy to come down from the ranch a couple of mornings a week if she thought it would be helpful. Within a few months we were building a home near town, and the medical work had developed into a twenty-four-hour-a-day, seven-day-a-week proposition.

After a few years I found, to my joy, that village practice is different from a practice in the city. I've driven on back roads in blizzards and whiteouts to make house calls on friends and neighbors. On summer days we've ridden together in the choking dust behind their cows and calves on the way to the mountain meadows. I've shared the loneliness of isolation and seen their stoic resignation to nature's forces. I've treated their cuts and bloody lips from barroom brawls, and reduced and cast their broken bones when they've been bucked off a horse or smashed by a bull in the rodeo ring. We've been together in their homes, by a young mother's bed as she cradles her newborn, and by the old four-poster where Grandpa is dying. We've been angry and sad, happy and relieved together.

Maybe it's because I am seventy-six, but I spend a lot of time thinking about how we take care of our old folk. The way our people die is a litmus paper for how we live as sons and daughters, as well as physicians. Our patients do not expect to live forever. Some are ready to die—want to die—before death finally comes. Most dread the time when they cannot do for themselves and think for themselves. They fear their pain will not be controlled, and they are terrified by treatments that sometimes prolong the agony of living, but do little to smooth the way toward a peaceful death. Our nursing homes are filled with miserable, alienated people who, in the words of a young woman physician, represent the defeats of our technical victories.

We have been taught as doctors that death is defeat. Most of us older docs, when we were young and starry-eyed, thought of death as a personal adversary in our battles to keep patients alive. And that is fine. I hope that doctors taking care of my children and grandchildren will fight as hard as possible to keep them well and happy. But I also hope that as I reach that stage in my life when quality of living is more important than how long I hang in there, my doctor and family will act accordingly. Death is inevitable. A death, devoid of agony, occurring in a place of choice for me and my family, and my four-legged friends, can come as a blessed relief. I want to go like my friend Charlie, who lapsed quietly into a coma at home with his dog under the bed. Only my dog will be on the bed beside me.

Over the past few years most of my patients have become "senior citizens," but then so have I. The stories that follow are about some of us.

CHAPTER 21

Fred

IHAD A PATIENT called Fred, an old hunting guide. He lived in Daniel, a spot on the map next to the Green River, twenty-two miles north of Big Piney on Highway 189, which continues north through the Hoback Canyon to Jackson Hole and the Grand Tetons. A brass plaque on a big rock in a grove of cottonwoods proclaims that this was where the first rendezvous was held between Indians and mountain men.

The Daniel General Store sells the best steaks in the county. The only other public establishment, besides the small post office, is the Green River Bar across the street, a log pub with its own paperback library and reading room. The hosts and owners are Pat and Hack Walker. Hack flew B-24s during the Second World War. The Walkers watch over some of the old-timers who live in cabins not far from the saloon. Joe Hausen is one of these. He was a great reader and his collection of paperbacks started the library.

The Green River breaks up into several meandering channels as it comes through Daniel. The eastern branches run through the Quarter Circle Five ranch, owned by a California family. Gnarled cottonwoods shade the cattle grazing in lush meadows. A village doc can get permission to fish there.

Fred lived in a scruffy old trailer not far from the rock and its plaque. He had lung cancer. My policy was, and still is, to see patients in their homes as often as necessary when they arrive at the end of their lives. My nurse, Deanne, and I do this together. Often we charge nothing for these calls, which is about as close as Medicare comes to paying anyway. The government has no billing codes for nonprocedural, compassionate care of a terminal patient, or for comfort given to a devastated family.

On a fall day, just before the start of hunting season, I drove over to Daniel and, turning into Darlene's Camper Court, parked next to Fred's trailer, the only one there. Bag in hand, I climbed the three rough steps he had hammered together under the narrow door. It was time to sit down with him and have a talk about his disease and his options. I pushed on the doorbell, which didn't work, and walked in. Fred was lying on a cot with a faded army blanket across his middle. He was surrounded by his hunting gear: well-used packsaddles, harnesses, tools, cans of nails and staples. Crumpled clothes were scattered everywhere. The place was a mess except for his guns, which stood neatly in an oak cabinet with brass fittings.

"Hello, Doc," he rasped. "Take that stuff off the chair and sit down."

"How's it going, Fred?" I asked.

"Great," said the old guide.

He looked terrible. His gray hair was uncombed, and a strand stuck to the sallow skin of his wrinkled forehead. He was wasting away.

As I wrapped my fingers around his wrist to check his pulse, he propped himself up on an elbow and started to cough—a deep, chest-rattling cough that squeezed the air out of his lungs in long, painful wheezes. He spat into a paper towel and lay back, his face a dusky blue, gasping for air. I reached across him and turned on the oxygen, then slipped the plastic tubing over his head and placed the prongs in his nostrils. After a little while his breathing became more regular and the lines of pain on his face and around his eyes relaxed.

"Thanks, Doc."

"Let me see what you coughed up."

He opened his fist, and I took the crumpled paper and saw a big glob of green phlegm streaked with bright red blood. Stepping into the bathroom, I dropped the paper towel into an overflowing garbage bag, then ran the hot water and wet a towel. I sat back down and washed off his face. He liked that.

I watched him as he lay on his back with his eyes closed. The coughing episode had, for the moment, cleared his "bronchials," as he called them. A truck roared by on the highway, and Darlene's dog yipped as it chased a rabbit into the sage. The only sounds in the trailer were Fred's breathing and the oxygen softly hissing into his nose. Outside, framed by the long window near the door, the leaves on the cottonwoods were bright yellow, some floating to the ground on a mountain breeze. Others had almost covered the empty cans of Coke and Coors dropped by tourists as they stood enjoying the unspoiled country where years ago trappers and Sioux had dropped their empty bottles of whiskey and broken arrowheads. Off in the pastures of the Quarter Circle Five, I could see the hay stacked for the winter and cows were calling to their calves, now old enough, after a summer in the mountains, to be a little independent.

I checked Fred's heart rate and pressure while a thermometer I'd stuck under his tongue was cooking. His pulse was up to 110; blood pressure okay. I pulled the thermometer out of his mouth; it read 100. I wiped it off with alcohol and put it and the other things back in my bag.

"Now, Fred, we have to talk."

"Shoot, Doc. I think I know what you're gonna say, and if I'm right the answer is no." He closed his eyes again.

"Fred, you have a pretty bad tumor in your lung. It's

plugging up some of your smaller bronchial tubes so that mucus in your lung has a hard time getting out. As I told you a couple of days ago, when mucus can't get out it gets infected and that makes pus and makes you cough the way you do. That's why I gave you those antibiotic pills to take last time. You have been taking one of those capsules four times a day, haven't you?"

"Sure, Doc."

I looked around but didn't see the pills. "If you want, I can send you to the hospital, where they can give you some X-ray treatments to shrink up the tumor and make you feel better."

"You can't take care of me here?" Half question, half statement.

"Sure I can. But I can't do anything about the tumor."

The old guide looked out of the window, thought for a while, then turned back to me. "When I was in there before, they told me that the X-ray treatment might shrink down the tumor for a little while—not for very long, and that the treatment might make me sick in other ways."

"That's true."

He looked directly at me. "I've had a good life, Doc. I've got no regrets. I don't want to go to no hospital." I nodded my acceptance. His old icebox turned on. It hummed and rattled in the background. Neither of us spoke for a while.

Darlene, who ran the trailer court, brought him one hot meal a day. As far as he was concerned, that was enough. His eating arrangements were simple. He had cereal and coffee out of a tin cup in the morning. In the evening he ate his dinner off the glossy pages of a Sears catalog. After each meal he tore off the page and was ready for the next one without having to wash dishes.

"You know, Doc, all I really want to do is go up to Gun Sight Pass one more time and watch my elk go by. Can you give me the strength to do that?"

I thought for a moment. "Fred, my wife makes a meat broth with some stuff called Bovril. She adds all sorts of her own mixings. It has everything in it. It'll make hair grow on a billiard ball."

He chuckled.

"I'll bring you some in a thermos every other day, and we'll see about getting you up to the pass."

Tine's broth, although never approved by the Food and Drug Administration, had been good medicine for many people, including me, over the years. Once, in Zaire, the Chinese ambassador had a rough bout of diarrhea that had left him dry and done in. I had given him the usual medicines, but it was Tine's broth that had him back on his feet quickly. He came to our house in the paratrooper camp a week or so later and brought, by way of thanks, cartons of Chinese cigarettes and boxes of tea.

Fred looked forward to Tine's broth. He sat on the edge of the cot and told me some of his hunting stories as he sipped from the plastic top of the thermos. Mostly he had hunted alone, carefully and thoughtfully, killing only what he needed for meat, like the bears and coyotes. But he had to guide to make a living. When he was through drinking he handed me the cup.

"This stuff's a hell of a lot better than all those pills you give me, Doc. Thank her, will ya?" I did.

Fred died peacefully in his sleep a few weeks later. He never saw his elk, but he never lost the hope that he might.

CHAPTER 22

Joyce

IN THE COURSE of twenty-four years of medical practice in Wyoming, I have frequently been asked by the family to give the eulogy at a patient's funeral. Meeting with the families to listen to happy memories of their loved ones have been times to celebrate life in the midst of death. Sometimes, as with Joyce, her own words brought a sense of reality and peace at the thought of my own mortality.

Joyce's life was defined by her great energy, her big heart, especially for children and the occasional "big-eye little-eye look," so familiar to her kids, which cut through nonsense or unacceptable behavior like a hot knife through butter.

She worked in the school lunch room for eighteen years. She loved all kids, even naughty kids, and squirted them with a red string from a ketchup bottle to get their attention and make them laugh. If a youngster lacked money for lunch, she would chip in and was always paid back by the kid. She thought it wrong to charge for food that would be thrown away. She often had the highest percentage in the state of students in her lunch room.

Nedra Aliff said, "I worked with Joyce for two years at the high school lunch room. She made it the best job I ever had. The kids loved and respected her. They called her 'Aunt Joyce.' During Spirit Week, she insisted we dress up for the theme of each day. We were asked to judge the skits at the last day assembly, and of course we couldn't just wear our work clothes to do this. She made long black robes for us. We wore string mops rolled up with juice cans for wigs so we would look like official judges.

The next year we were Judge Roy Bean's brothers. We wore Western jeans, shirts, boots, old hats and gun holsters. The kids loved it. Joyce had a wonderful outlook on life, a great attitude, a terrific sense of humor. We will all miss her."

According to Jeannie Lockwood: "Joyce had problems with turning mixers on full speed when they were full of pudding! She usually wore what she was cooking."

Darlene Holgate: "She loved all children and would sneak them treats like cookies and hot rolls."

Joyce won the respect of the kids and, with the same big-eye, little-eye look, had them saying "thank you" and "please." All those who worked with her remember when she was cleaning out the depths of the huge stew pot they call the "witches' pot" and fell in head first with her feet waving in the breeze.

In her home, there was always enough to feed an extra kid or the strays that her husband, Spike, brought to the family table. Joyce took on the Cub Scouts in LaBarge, determined to teach them about fire safety and how to build a campfire to roast wieners and marshmallows. She gathered the rocks, started a fire, and the cookout was underway when a gust of wind carried sparks into the grass and the blaze that followed called out the LaBarge fire trucks. She never did live that down.

When Spike and Joyce lived at Dry Piney Creek, their house was next to a rough dirt road used by Belco oilfield hands. About that time, Louie Dapra gave Spike a long-haired dog called Handsome who liked to chase the trucks. On a hot day, the truckers drove by the house with their windows down to catch a little air. Along came a good-looking young fellow, driving like a bat out of hell. Handsome took out after him followed by Joyce shouting at the top of her lungs, "Handsome, you little son of a bitch, get back here!" The driver, I gather, rolled up his window and put the pedal to the metal (as the kids would say).

More recently, Dr. Vilija Avizonis, Radiation Oncologist at LDS Hospital, said "Of all the patients we see regardless of their situation, and hers was one of the most serious, Joyce was always pleasant and had a smile for everyone, and her smile made you smile back."

In the last few months and weeks, everyone who visited Joyce and Spike went in sad and came out amazed and uplifted.

When my time comes, I hope to have half the faith, the courage, the humor that Joyce had at the end of her life. She is a remarkable example of a woman with a huge heart, irrepressible humor and an unfettered spirit. Never an ounce of self-pity, but constant amazement that so many wrote to her and came to visit. To have the whole family together for their recent forty-fifth wedding anniversary meant everything to Joyce and Spike.

The battle we fight is not with death, it's how we die that counts. Joyce wrote a poem a little over two months before she died. She called it "The Battle."

> Well, it's almost over
> This battle that I've fought.
> I keep my head up high
> But now it seems for naught.
>
> We poked me and we prodded
> With shots and pills and rays.
> We all geared up to beat this—
> But we're down to counting days!
>
> For the rotten thing has traveled
> Oh, that filthy little fellow
> Up there in my head he is
> That Spike says is full of Jello.

So, God, I need to ask You,
Because You know I've done my best,
That You're going to be there for me
As I come to You for rest.

And I look forward to being there
With my loved ones gone before
So, now I have to ask myself—

Did I lose the battle? Or have I won the war?

You won the war, Joyce. You showed us how to live and love all out, and taught us how to die with grace and courage.

CHAPTER 23

Chuck

D EANNE and I refer to a few of our old-time patients as "TNTs"—total non-turkeys. Harriett Chrisman and her brother, Chuck, were two of our favorites. Chuck always accompanied Harriett to the clinic for an occasional checkup or minor medical problem. The first time Chuck came in for himself he had a thickening of his lower lip.

"Howaya, Doc?"

"Great, Chuck. What about you?"

"Just walkin' around savin' funeral expenses." The peak of his Pillsbury cap was off center, giving his blue eyes and the upper part of his face a small-boy look. But the gray stubble in the creases next to his long nose and the hollows in his cheeks showed his age. His lower lip was pushed out in an uncharacteristic pout.

Many years ago Chuck had come to terms with the fact that his sister ran the Mule Tree. He'd been raised to do chores and was a "good hand." Harriett's cooking—mashed potatoes and gravy next to a fist-size chunk of well-done beef—made up for a lot of things. And when she wasn't reading or "tootin' up the accounts," she baked biscuits angels would fight over.

I pulled on rubber gloves and grasped Chuck's lower lip and gently ran a finger over the swelling. The old man rolled his eyes up to Deanne. "Wha' price ya gettin' for your calves?"

She laughed. "You'll have to ask Allen."

I released the lip and Chuck wiped saliva off his chin with the back of his hand. "Ya wouldn't tell me anyway, wouldja?"

"That lump is smaller and softer than it was a couple of weeks ago. I think we can let it go and check it again in a month, unless you're worried about it."

"I ain't worried about it if you're not, Doc. When ya comin' fishin'?"

"Any day now."

"That's what ya always say." He turned to Deanne. "Make him take a day off and go fishin'."

"I will. Any day now," she repeated, handing him an appointment card for a month. "Call us if your lip bleeds again."

"Sure will if ya tell me how much ya got for your calves."

Deanne laughed and pushed him gently toward the door.

Chuck and Harriett lived on an old ranch on LaBarge Creek. They had a dog called Roscoe with a chewed-up ear. Harriett was the brains and Chuck the brawn of the outfit. Whenever he talked about her, he'd tell me, "She's the boss." And that was all right with him because she took care of the money and "fed good." But the old lady lost her hearing and her sight and eventually died of emphysema in a hospital. The floor staff refused to let Chuck sit by her bedside for more than an hour a day.

"Why wouldn't they let you stay with her?" I asked.

"I s'pose because I tromped in with muddy boots and asked too many goddamn questions. I don' really know. They told me it was hospital regulations."

After his sister died, Chuck plodded along doing his chores like a robot. He drove his old pickup to my office every week. He wasn't sick in the usual way, but he certainly had a broken heart. He'd come in and just sit there shaking his head and say, "Sure do miss her. So does Roscoe."

We'd talk about Harriett, her keen mind, sharp

tongue, and her "meat-gravy-mashed-putater" dinners. A light went on in the old boy when he talked about his sister.

"She had no tolerance for fools and fussy women. No, sir. And I sure knew when to keep my mouth shut. Early on she taught me, if ya want to eat right don't hassle the cook."

I looked at him as he leaned his thin elbows on my desk. There wasn't much to say. I just listened even during the long silences. And that meant I closed the door to the office and turned off the phone. Deanne knew we weren't to be interrupted.

The meetings all ended the same way. He'd stand up and lean on my desk and look at me with wet eyes.

"It's the evenings that are the worst, Doc."

I'd put my arm around his shoulders and he'd say, "Thanks. You're a helluva doctor."

And all I'd done was listen.

CHAPTER 24

Toni

THE GREEN RIVER VALLEY in western Wyoming lies at seven thousand feet in a triangle formed by the Wind River range on the northeast and the Wyoming range to the west. Gannett Peak, rising 13,800 feet in the northern "Windies," pokes its sharp, snow-clad summit into a dark blue sky and points north to the Grand Tetons. The base of the triangle is the beginning of the Great Red Desert of flat sand buttes, badlands, and roving herds of antelope and wild horses that stretches south to Colorado.

In the middle of the valley, twenty miles north of Big Piney, sits the Dapra ranch. Louie Dapra and his wife, Toni, have lived there for twelve years. They turned a run-down outfit of three hundred deeded acres into an efficient cow-calf operation, which at least paid for itself and sometimes turned a small profit. Louie's father came over from France. His name was Du Pré—from the meadow, but he changed the spelling to Dapra with a long *a*—simpler and more suitable for the mountains.

Toni, whose given name was Leona, taught school. The two of them met and were married. They had one son, who was killed in a car accident. Although they had no family in the county, they were loved and respected by many friends.

I first met the Dapras when I stopped at the ranch to see Toni in the middle of May. Both were in their early sixties. Her neighbor, my nurse Deanne's sister-in-law, had called to ask if we could see Toni now that she was back from the hospital in Jackson.

Before the house call, I had been in touch with Martha Stearn, a thoroughly competent and compassionate

183

physician in Jackson. She sent me a copy of Toni's records. Eight years ago Toni was treated in Salt Lake City with chemotherapy and radiation for a malignant lymphoma in her abdomen. Although she was desperately sick during the treatments, the tumor apparently melted away, and Toni lived seven years with few medical problems.

During those years Louie worked long hours in the oil field to supplement their ranch income and help cover Toni's medical bills. Toni helped him with the cattle. Every day the stock had to be fed, even in howling blizzards when the temperature was minus thirty. The Dapras' hard work made it possible for them to pay off their debts and look forward to some travel and fun together.

Then, during the middle of 1987, Toni's abdominal pains recurred. At first, she considered them a nuisance. She had a lot to do and paid little attention to them. However, during the winter, the pains became more frequent and more severe.

By March of 1988, she had no appetite, was frequently nauseated, and a definite and painful swelling had appeared in the upper part of her abdomen on the left side. She was admitted to the hospital in Jackson Hole. A CAT scan revealed a huge spleen. She underwent a splenectomy for relief of the pain, but the lymphoma had returned with a vengeance.

Over the next two months she lost twenty-three pounds and became progressively weaker. The pain in her abdomen was constant, and in the morning, after a night of suffering, it was especially severe under her left rib cage.

Toni was readmitted to the hospital. The upper left side of her abdominal cavity was filled with recurrent malignant tissue that invaded her left chest, producing large quantities of fluid in her left pleural cavity. With her lung compressed by the fluid, her breathing became difficult and painful. Neither Toni nor the doctors in Jackson and Salt Lake felt that further chemotherapy or radiation would be of any use. Toni wanted to go home.

Thursday, May 19. First house call with Deanne.

We drove to the ranch to talk about what we might do to keep Toni comfortable. Deanne had known the Dapras for a long time. Dea is the fourth generation of her family in Big Piney and sometimes I think she's related to most of the people in the valley. After high school Deanne enrolled in nursing but did little with her RN degree until she and her husband, Allen, saw their children well on the way through high school. In 1980, she came to work for me. After polishing her nursing skills, she became a partner in the care of our patients. Deanne has a warm heart and commonsense authority so necessary for a good nurse. She's a rock with a smile. When we trimmed down our practice to two and a half days a week in the office, she put a big purple badge on my desk: SEMI-RETIRED AND SEMI-IMPOSSIBLE.

As we drove up to the Dapras' ranch house, Edna, Toni's sister from St. Louis, came out to meet us at the gate. Toni's Norwegian elkhound, Zack, barked but let us go up the steps to the little mudroom and the front door. As Edna led us into the living room she told us that Louie was out fixing fence and wouldn't be back until later. The room was neat and comfortable: big picture windows framing a view of hay fields with the Windies in the background.

An oxygen concentrator was humming next to the hallway leading to the back of the house. Edna led the way and we followed the plastic tube past the kitchen, down the hall, and into the bedroom on the left.

"Here's Deanne and the doctor," she announced.

"Hi, Toni. Glad to see you home," said Dea. "This is Dr. Close."

I went over to the bed and we shook hands. "Nice to meet you, Toni." Her grip was firm, and her dark blue eyes were strong and looked me square in the eye.

"Thank you for coming," she answered, a little short of breath. She was lying in a big walnut bed, propped up with pillows. Dea checked her pressure and pulse. I sat on a chair that Edna brought in from the kitchen.

Toni was certainly short of breath, even with the oxygen she was getting through nasal prongs. The loose skin on her arms and neck, the hollows under her cheekbones, and her deep eye sockets were evidence of her weight loss from the cancer. Her sparse gray hair was flattened in the back from the pressure of the pillows, but it was short and neat in front. Her face showed few wrinkles except for smile lines radiating from her eyes. The skin over her forehead was tight and damp with sweat. Altogether, she had the look of a strong-minded, capable ranch wife. She would have been strong-bodied but for the cancer. Deanne took off the cuff, stuffing it back into the bag. Toni braced herself against the pillows with her elbows and looked at me expectantly.

"I had a good talk with Dr. Stearn and have gone through the records she sent me. Dea and I will do everything we can to keep you comfortable. How are you doing right now?"

"I'm okay. Just pain in my chest," she said, between short breaths. She put her hand over her left rib cage and tried to take a deep breath, but winced and dropped her hand with a quick smile through the pain.

"Hurts," she said.

"Let me take a look."

Toni hiked herself up on the pillows. "I haven't had a bowel movement in three days."

"I'll check that, too."

Dea put her arm around Toni's shoulders and helped her sit up so I could listen to her lungs. It didn't take long. Half her lung cavity on the left was filled with fluid. Gently we laid her back on her pillows. I felt her abdomen. It was distended, and in the area just below her left rib cage, I could feel the tumor. It was hard and tender.

"We need to be sure you don't have a rectal impaction," I said, looking at Dea. She nodded. "Edna and I will step out for a second."

A moment later Deanne opened the door. "No impaction."

Back in the room, I sat down on the edge of the bed.

Toni asked, "What do you think?"

"I think your pain and shortness of breath are coming from the tumor and the fluid it's making around your left lung. But you know that already, don't you?" I said, feeling my way.

"Yes," she said.

I watched her taking short, rapid breaths. She was hunched over on her right side. Although her face reflected suffering, her expression held no self-pity.

"Can you do anything about this pain?" she asked, putting her left hand over her chest.

"We can increase your pain medicine to make you more comfortable."

"Okay, but what about my bowels?"

"You're on lots of stool softener for that, but the pain medicine is probably slowing things down. How much water are you drinking?" I asked her.

"Not much. I don't like water."

"You can drink anything you want as long as it's wet: tea, coffee, juice, beer, wine, whiskey—probably bourbon for a rancher. Anything! The more you drink, the easier it will be for your bowels to work. You're not eating very much, so it's really important to drink lots of liquids."

Holding the nasal tongs of the oxygen catheter, she turned her head to give me a straight look and smiled. "Louie and I always had a highball at the end of the day before supper."

"Great. Have one with him again," I said.

"Okay," she said, with a little chuckle.

I got up. "We'll check you again in three days. I'll go over your medicines with Edna and increase the dose of your pain pills." I paused. "We'll stick with you, Toni. I don't know how much time you have left. Nobody knows that. But the most important thing right now is that you are where you want to be, in your own home, with your sister and husband taking good care of you. We'll do what's necessary so that you will not have big pain. Dea and I can come anytime. Just call us."

"Thanks, Doctor. You won't forget about my bowels, will you?"

"I won't forget," I said, shaking hands as we left.

Sunday, May 22, 10 A.M. House call with Deanne.

Toni was uncomfortable. No bowel movement for six days. Her mouth was very dry. Although the medicine was clearly keeping her pain under control, it was adding to her constipation. Edna said she had been drinking more, and except for the constipation, she was doing better.

Her abdomen was moderately distended and slightly tender all over. I put my stethoscope on her tummy. The bowel sounds were active—and some high-pitched—but not like they are when the bowel is trying to push gas through an obstruction. But was pressure from the tumor on her colon contributing to a partial obstruction? The remainder of the exam was unchanged; still a lot of fluid in her left chest.

I asked Deanne to give her three suppositories followed by an enema. While she was doing that I went out in the kitchen with Louie. He'd brewed coffee.

"What do you think, Doc?" he asked.

"We've got to get her bowels to move, Louie, or she might get into real trouble. I don't think she's obstructed, but that's something we have to consider with all that's going on inside her. Let's see if the suppositories and the enema work."

"Sure glad you could come out, Doc."

"I hope we can get things moving," I replied.

"She sure doesn't want to go back to the hospital."

"I know, Louie. I hope we can continue to take care of her here."

Jackson is seventy miles from the Dapra ranch. The nearest medical center is Salt Lake, two hundred miles away. We always have to keep in mind the distances and the difficulty of transportation, especially if a spring snowstorm roars down from the mountains.

"More coffee, Doc?"

"No thanks, Louie."

Dea came in. "Any luck?" I asked.

"Not really."

"Any gas?"

"A little."

"What now, Doc?" asked Louie.

"Let's get her to drink as much as possible. We'll see what happens through the day. Maybe you or Edna can call me around four o'clock this afternoon."

"Okay," said Louie.

I went back to the bedroom and encouraged Toni to drink at least one and a half quarts of any liquid.

Phone call at 4 P.M.

Edna reported that Toni still had not moved her bowels. Having mulled over the situation most of the afternoon, I felt the evidence was against obstruction. I asked Edna to give her four tablespoons of milk of magnesia.

"Four tablespoons?" asked Edna.

"Right. Four tablespoons," I confirmed.

Phone call at 10 P.M. I had just gone to sleep.

"Dr. Close, this is Edna. Toni is vomiting."

My first thought was, Oh, my God, she was obstructed! "I'll come right away."

I dressed quickly and drove out, feeling scared and worried about whether I had done the right thing. Maybe I should have dodged the issue and forced her to go to the hospital. What would people think if I had mistreated a bowel obstruction with a big dose of milk of magnesia? There might be the inevitable questions from the family— not Louie or Edna necessarily, but the other members of the family back east. Would they be angry or upset and talk about the primitive medicine practiced in the boonies?

I could hear a lawyer's voice booming in the court as he held up a bottle of milk of magnesia. *Dr. Close, I assume you have read this label?* "Do not take any laxative if abdominal pain, nausea, vomiting, or change in bowel habits persist over two weeks, or if rectal bleeding or kidney disease are present."

If she was obstructed, I would have no choice but to call the ambulance and send her to the hospital. The obstruction would have to be relieved surgically or she would die horribly. What if she refused to go? What would Louie and Edna say? I had the impression Edna thought four tablespoons of milk of magnesia was a lot. Maybe she was right. If Toni was vomiting, I'd have to give her IVs. I certainly couldn't let her die of simple dehydration.

As I drove the twenty miles in the dark to the Dapras, I thought of other patients I had taken care of in equally difficult and critical times. About a year back, when one of my old-timers had been dying in the nursing home, the family had been divided into two camps. One group wanted me to follow the patient's wishes to keep him comfortable and let him die. The other group had wanted the patient transferred to a big medical center where all sorts of diagnostic procedures and interventions could be done. I spent hours with both groups listening to their views and answering their questions. The patient's wishes were my guide. The whole thing was unpleasant, to put it mildly. Whispers of litigation tied my gut into painful knots.

I was not used to the threat of being sued by patients or their families. In New York in the fifties, and certainly in Africa, suing and "sewage insurance," as some of us called it, were not factors in practice. A doctor was expected to be polite and knowledgeable and do his best. Honest mistakes were made and regretted, but it was rare that a doctor was considered to have acted maliciously or against the best interests of the patient.

I pulled into the ranch at 10:30 P.M. Edna and Louie were waiting at the door.

"Thanks for coming right away, Doc," said Louie.

"Let's see how she's doing."

Toni looked awful and was breathing with great difficulty and pain. Her face and hair were drenched with sweat. She could not find a comfortable position. Louie brought a chair and I sat down next to the bed. He stood in the doorway and Edna stood at the foot of the bed. The two little lamps on the bedside tables were the only light in the room.

"Nothing's come out . . . and the pain's really bad. It's no use, Doc, I think I'm going to give up," Toni said, in small gasps.

"How much have you vomited?" I asked her.

She pointed to Edna who showed me a basin with a small amount of yellow bile in it. I leaned over and sniffed it. No fecal material. That was a relief.

I put my hand on her wrist and counted her pulse— 112.

"Edna, could you give me a warm washcloth, please?" I asked.

I wiped Toni's forehead and the corners of her eyes, then folded it over and wiped the gray, caked saliva from her lips.

"Giving up won't change anything, Toni. You'll go when your time comes. If giving up would take away the pain and make you better, I'd be all for it. But giving up will only make it harder for Edna and Louie and me to take care of you. I'm not doing anything to prolong things," I said very quietly.

"I know, Doc," she whispered.

I felt her abdomen. It was bloated, a little worse than this morning. Gently I tapped her abdominal wall with a finger. She was tender in the right lower quadrant. When I pressed a little and quickly withdrew my hand, she winced with pain. She had a little rebound tenderness, which meant that things were tight and irritated in that area. I took out my stethoscope, put the bell under my arm for a moment to warm it up, and laid it on her tummy. The bowel sounds were hyperactive and there were occasional high-pitched gurgles.

"Have you been able to keep anything down since I was here this morning?" I asked.

Edna replied for her. "She's had a cup of coffee, three large glasses of water, and a little cereal for lunch. She kept all that down."

"I do not want to go to a hospital," said Toni firmly, holding her hand over her left chest.

"I know, Toni. But here is the situation," I replied. "You haven't had a bowel movement for over six days. You have started to vomit, and your pain is worse than it was this morning. I do not think you are obstructed, but I cannot be sure. The tumor may be putting enough pressure on your colon to make it hard for stuff to go through."

"What do you want to do?" she asked.

"I'd give anything to get an X ray of your tummy. It would really help me to know what to do."

"Where would you do that?"

"In the hospital."

She looked at me, closed her eyes tightly, and shook her head slowly.

"Toni, if you're obstructed then we will have to do something about it surgically or we won't be able to do anything about the pain. It would be a hell of a way to die. I'm not looking for something to prolong your suffering but for something that will relieve it."

Her pain was obvious, but she continued shaking her head.

I persisted. "I told you I would respect your wishes. But I must tell you what I think, then you have to make up your own mind."

Louie had pulled up a straight-backed chair to my left. He was sitting with his elbows on his knees, his hands clasped together, looking down at his boots. Edna's fingers were curling and uncurling on the footboard of the old bed. The only sound in the room was Toni's rapid, shallow breathing.

After a little while Toni said, "Give me a few more hours, Doc. And give me something for the pain."

I looked at Louie. He shrugged, then nodded.

Edna said, "If that's what she wants . . ."

"Okay, Toni. I'll give you a shot of morphine and Compazine. That will take away the pain and the nausea."

Edna helped her roll over on her side and I gave her the shot.

"I'll stay here until you're asleep," I said.

She closed her eyes and waited for relief. In twenty minutes she was sound asleep, breathing more normally, and the pain lines in her face had eased. Louie sat watching Toni as she slept.

"How are you doing, Louie?" I whispered.

He looked at me for a moment and said, "I feel so helpless." He wiped his eyes and face with a red handkerchief.

"There's nothing any of us can do except keep her comfortable."

"I guess that's right, Doc. But it's so tough. Here we were expecting to be able to be together and travel around now that everything is finally paid up, and this happens . . . and there's nothing I can do, nothing at all."

I looked at him, feeling his pain and hopelessness.

"Ya want some coffee now, Doc?"

"Sure, Louie, that would be great."

It was a little after midnight when I left. Louie walked me to the door. Zack was waiting for Louie to come out to him.

"Great little dog he is. Goes everywhere with me, but Toni doesn't let him in the house," said Louie, patting the dog on the head.

"Call me, Louie."

"I will. Thanks."

Monday, May 23, 6 A.M.

The phone rang.

"Hey, Doc, this is Louie. At three this morning her bowels really moved—the biggest I've ever seen. She feels much better."

"That's great news." Relief surged through me. "Why didn't you call me at three?"

"Well, I thought you needed the sleep," he replied.

"Thanks, Louie. Boy, am I relieved."

"So am I. And so is she!"

Monday, May 23, 4:30 P.M. House call.

Toni looks better, feels better, and her morale is definitely brighter. She has some nausea if she eats too fast or too much, but she has been drinking lots of fluids. I did the usual examinations.

"Are you getting out of bed?" I asked.

"Only to go to the bathroom."

"I think she's trying to save her energy," said Edna.

"I'm glad things are on the up-and-up, Toni. I think some of your medicines may be making you a little sick at your stomach. We'll stop everything except the pain pills. I want you to take one every six hours, by the clock. You will have less pain if you take the pill regularly, not just when you need it."

She nodded and smiled.

"Eat anything you want," I continued. "I don't think you'll be as nauseated if you eat small amounts frequently. And keep up the good fluid intake. And, Toni, get out of bed. Living each day as fully as you can with what energy you have is the thing to do. Don't try to save your energy, use it. Get up several times a day and go into the living room, and go out on your porch if the weather is good. I think your dog is missing you. If you won't let him in the house, then go out and see him."

She gave me one of those looks teachers give when you've said enough.

"Anyway, don't be afraid of doing too much."

Over the next few days I did another house call and stayed in touch by phone. Toni's pain was under good control with her medicine taken regularly. She was getting out of bed more and her bowels were moving normally. The only problem was that she was getting more fluid in her left chest and breathing was becoming more difficult.

Monday, May 30. Memorial Day, 10 A.M. House call with Deanne.

Toni was very short of breath. When she spoke she could only get out a few words at a time. Three quarters of her left chest was filled with fluid.

Dea and I helped her out of bed to straddle a straight-backed chair with her arms folded over the back. Using a very small needle, I infiltrated local anesthetic into her left chest wall below the shoulder blade. I pushed the medicine in slowly to deaden the tissues between the skin and the inside of her chest cavity. Then, with a larger needle on a syringe, I went through the anesthetized tissue and withdrew 1,200 cc of yellow chest fluid. It took a while because we were using a 20-cc syringe. Dea kept one hand on Toni's shoulder and in the other held a basin for the fluid I was removing.

"There's one thing I'd like to do," said Toni, breathing a little better as the fluid came out.

"What's that?" asked Dea.

"I'd like to plant one more bush in the hedge around the house. I've put in one each year for the past seven years."

"Great, we'll aim for that," said Dea. "What kind are they?"

"Honeysuckle."

"I bet they're beautiful in the spring."

After the initial needle stick, Toni felt nothing, and after the fluid had been removed, she was much more comfortable and her breathing was almost normal.

On June 7, we took out another 1,400 cc of fluid from Toni's pleural cavity with the same relief of her breathing as before.

Saturday, June 11, 10 A.M. House call with Deanne.

Toni collapsed on the way to the bathroom. She was not hurt but was certainly getting weaker. Her breathing was even more difficult and painful than before.

We walked into her room. She was lying in bed, propped up by a bunch of pillows. The oxygen machine was going at three liters and she was breathing very fast, struggling for air with each breath.

I sat down next to the bed. "How's the pain, Toni?"

"Pretty good," she whispered, between gasps.

"But the breathing is too tough now, isn't it?"

She nodded with a fleeting smile.

"Let me take a quick look and listen."

Dea put her arm around Toni's shoulders and helped her pull away from the pillows. The right lung sounded normal. The left had no breath sounds at all, and in the upper third there was that hollow sound that comes with air in the pleural cavity. It was clear that she had another chestful of fluid with air riding above it, probably from our previous chest taps. At the base of her neck, her trachea was pushed over to the right by the pressure of the air and water in her left chest cavity.

"Toni, I think the time has come to get you back to the

hospital, where we can do an X ray and maybe put a little tube into your chest to take out the air and water that's making it so hard for you to breathe."

She looked at me steadily and with great difficulty asked, "They won't do anything else except help me breathe, will they?"

"No, Toni, they won't."

"All right, Doc," she said, and closed her eyes.

I went into the kitchen with Louie. We sat down at the kitchen table facing each other. "I'm sure glad you talked her into going back up, Doc. I can't stand to see her suffer."

"I think she'll be much more comfortable up there. They can help with her breathing. Louie, you've done a wonderful job taking care of her."

"Thanks, Doc."

I called Dr. Stearn and told her that Toni made me promise that nothing except the relief of her breathing would be done in the hospital. She assured me that she would respect those wishes.

Toni was in the hospital for six days. Fluid was removed from her chest, but this time she got little relief and became weaker and weaker. The pain in her left side became more severe. She was given morphine, which she could control herself through her IV, and her pain stayed under control. During the last two days she was too weak to dose herself and the nurses helped her. At the end of June she lapsed into a coma and died peacefully during the night.

Two days after the funeral Deanne bought two honeysuckle bushes at Burney's, our general merchandise store, and drove out to the Dapra ranch. Edna was in the house. Louie was out working.

"Toni didn't have a chance to plant honeysuckles this spring, so Dr. Close and I thought Louie might like these to put in the yard," said Dea, carrying the two young bushes up the steps and putting them on the porch by the front door.

While the two women were visiting in the living room, Louie came in from the fields and sat down.

"Hello, Deanne," he said. "What's in those buckets out on the porch?" Edna told Louie about the bushes.

"Thanks, Deanne," he said, "You've got a great memory. Toni sure loved those bushes, watered them all the time." He turned away. "I'll get the coffee going."

In September, the aspen turn golden and stand out against the dark green of the spruce and pine in the mountains. The foothills are quiet and peaceful and antelope herds with their young roam the benches. The deer and moose are still in the timber. The elk are higher, nearer the permanent snow line.

For many in this part of Wyoming, it is a favorite time. Ranching families slowly drive their cattle from the high mountain meadows to the home ranches for sorting and shipping to the markets in Iowa, Kansas, and Colorado.

Deanne, her husband, Allen, and their kids were pushing their cows down Cottonwood Road. Their daughter, Audrey, was in a pickup ahead of the herd. The truck's hazard lights were blinking and she was waving a red flag at any vehicle coming toward the cattle ambling down the road. The herd filled the highway and the ditches on both sides and were being urged on slowly by Allen, his other daughter, Marilyn, and son, Mack. Deanne brought up the rear in a pickup with red flags sticking out of the window to warn cars coming up from behind. A long trail of splattered cow pies on the road would certainly warn people that someone was moving cows up ahead, but the highway department required flaggers in front and behind.

Deanne was crawling along in low gear with the family's dinner on the seat next to her when she saw Louie's truck creeping toward her through the herd. When he came up to her they both stopped while the cattle and riders moved on slowly.

"How's it going?" asked Dea.

"I'm real glad to see you, Deanne. Been trying to call you and thank you for the honeysuckles. I planted 'em, and they've done real well."

"That's great. How are you doing?" she asked.

"Okay—I guess."

"Allen and I would love to see you. Could you come to dinner on Sunday?"

"Oh, I'd like that, Dea."

"Great. See you later, Louie. Gotta catch up with the cows."

"See ya soon," said Louie, with a big smile.

CHAPTER 25

Pete

PETE, a thin, ornery eighty-five-year-old cowboy fixated on his bowel functions, was spending the winter with his son in Idaho. Pete had emphysema, small-vessel intermittent claudication, and a tight aortic valve. He was also one of my few neurotic patients that hadn't been chased out of the mountains by our twenty-below winters. Sometime in January, his son called me to say that Pete had spit up a little blood; could I suggest a doctor in Salt Lake for him to see? My regular consultant, the sort of physician I would send my own family to, was out of town. I was put through to his partner—a man in his fifties who was a chest surgeon, cardiac surgeon, general surgeon, and vascular surgeon running a brand-new vascular lab. About ten days later he called me.

"Thank you for sending me that charming patient, Dr. Close."

"You mean Pete?"

"Right! Delightful old gentleman." I thought Pete must have gone through some sort of metamorphosis to be tagged "delightful," but I said nothing and urged him to tell me what he had found.

"We put him through the whole works. He has intermittent claudication—small vessel—and there's not too much we can do for that."

"I know. I walked him fifty yards over to the little movie house behind the clinic and came to the same conclusion. We call it the 'Flick Test.' What about his hemoptysis?"

"I scoped him and scanned him. He has a small, well-

201

differentiated adenocarcinoma in his left upper lobe, and aortic stenosis."

"Yes," I replied. "Since he can only walk small distances because of his claudication, his AS hasn't really been a problem. What do you have in mind for him?"

"Well." His tone of voice indicated that he was glad to be done with the preliminaries and ready to get down to business. "I am planning to give him a new aortic valve, and after he recovers from that, I will take out his left lung."

"Good God, man!" I exclaimed into the phone. "That's a hell of a lot of surgery for an old man who sits in a chair all day worrying about his bowels." There was a long silence at the other end.

"What would you suggest, Doctor?" he asked tightly.

"A little radiation to the well-differentiated tumor in his lung, and a discharge to the care of his sister, Ruby. She and her husband are ranchers. She'll take good care of him."

"Since you are the referring doctor, I will do what you want."

I thanked him and hung up, then called Ruby to brief her.

The last time I saw Pete he was sitting by a corner window in Ruby's kitchen watching the cows amble by.

"Ain't moved my bowels for a couple of days, Doc," he announced as I walked in. I was about to review the Metamucil—Colace—Haley's MO—prune-juice cocktail in his regimen, when Ruby pushed past me.

"Peter," she said, with her hands on her ample hips, "ya eat like a bird an' shit like a bird. That's your only problem."

Pete died sometime later, relatively happy and stuffed on Ruby's ranch cooking. The multifaceted surgeon, I am sure, found someone else to chip on.

CHAPTER 26

John

I STROLLED ALONG a small rocky stream John had favored, trying to recall the details of our time together. Scattered beams of evening sun filtered through ancient cottonwoods, as gnarled and timeworn as my old friend. The throaty calls of sandhill cranes in a pasture of new-cut hay rose above the rustle of leaves. Plenty of voices were there, but not John's. I climbed Dead Indian Dome and sat on one of nature's stools carved out of sandstone by wind and rain. The view of the valley seemed to clear my mind, and I pulled a pad out of my pack and jotted down what I remembered about John's last weeks.

When I first met John he was in his late seventies—a tall, gray-haired man who continued to fish in spite of high blood pressure, emphysema, and bad arthritis. His only real concern was that the pain in his crippled joints would progress to the point where he would be unable to wade a mountain stream, particularly in the early fall when the mosquitoes are killed off by the first frosts and the aspen turn yellow and quake among the spruce.

A few years later I sat at his bedside in the nursing home. He lay on his side, propped over with cushions along his back and between his swollen knees, his stubbled face half-buried in a pillow. I put my hand on his shoulder. After a moment he stirred slowly.

"Hi, John, how are you doing?" He shook his head.

I continued, "Is there anything I can do for you?"

He ran his tongue over dry lips, struggled to prop himself up on an elbow, and mumbled, "Sure, Doc. Same ol' thing. Give me a million."

"A million?" I handed him a glass of water. "For what?"

"I dunno. Dumb idea, I guess." This was the way most of our talks had started over the last month or so. He swallowed a couple of mouthfuls and handed back the glass. "Can't get out of bed, can't even go to the can without help, and I sure can't take it with me." He rolled painfully onto his back. I wrestled with his pillows and tucked one under his gray head. "Thanks, Doc. You're a good nurse." He wiggled his shoulders into the bedding and looked up at me. "Got a question for you."

"Shoot."

"What's your idea of heaven, Doc?"

I thought for a moment.

"A place with sage-covered hills where I can walk with every dog I've ever owned without getting short of breath. Mountain glades where they can run after rabbits but never catch them—where they play without fighting or chasing the game or the neighbor's cattle." He pointed to the water pitcher. I poured him another glassful. He drank half then made a face. "A little whiskey would sure make that taste better."

I nodded. "What do you think heaven will be like?"

"That's easy. A stream with sparkling water and the lazy bubbles of a feed line off some grassy bank where a big brown's waiting for my fly. A place where I can fish alone and never look at my watch or think of the end of summer." He closed his eyes and after a moment continued, "Sure hope Ethel makes it back soon."

"I can call her."

"Do it, Doc. I need to talk to her." He grabbed the bed rail and pulled himself back onto his side and, with a deep sigh, ended the conversation.

The next afternoon I drove over with Vengie, my shaggy black Bouvier, to see John. He was sitting up in bed, shaved, wearing bright blue pajamas.

"Hope you brought that fat check with you, Doc."

"Of course, John. Got it in my bag." I sat, and Vengie collapsed beside me to catch a nap. "Sure good to see you looking so perky."

"Had a great time with Ethel this morning. We haven't talked like that for years. Got everything straightened out."

I pulled a little flask of Jack Daniel's from my pocket and poured a dollop into his glass, topping it off with water. He took it from me and raised it in a salute. "Give that check to Ethel, Doc." He downed his drink and put the glass on the bedside table. "Thanks," he said, with a grin on his face. "That's much better." He relaxed into his pillows. "You know, Ethel always was more unselfish than me. I'd have made more people happy if I'd let her do what she wanted." He reached down and patted the dog. "He's the one you take fishing with you?"

"That's him."

"You must love him a lot."

"I do."

Most evenings after that Vengie and I sat with John for a while. And most of the time he slept. Once, he opened an eye and said, "It's nice to have you and your fishing dog just be here without asking all the time, 'How ya doin'?' " Ethel came regularly and worked quietly on her needlepoint. John had quit eating; we both felt he was just biding his time.

On one of our last visits Vengie was snoring peacefully with his rear end sticking out from under the bed. John was asleep on his side next to the rail. Suddenly the old man sputtered and coughed and opened his eyes.

"That dog of yours can sure pass gas."

"Sorry about that. I guess I've kind of gotten used to

it. Sorry to wake you up that way."

"I can think of worse ways. Anyway I wasn't sleeping, just thinking."

"Thinking what?"

"There's something I wish you'd do, Doc, but I'm pretty sure you won't."

"What's that?"

"Can't fish anymore. Can't eat or pee anymore, and even moving in bed hurts. Isn't there some way you can speed things up for me?"

"Can't do that, John. It's against the law."

"I figured you'd say that," he said, shaking his head.

I said, "If you were my windy old dog I could put you out of your misery. The way things are, I can be kinder to my dog than to you. But I promise I'm doing nothing to prolong things. I'm only trying to keep you comfortable."

"I can understand the tube in my bladder—beats the hell out of being wet all the time. And the sheepskin under my butt sure feels better than a rubber sheet. But how about those horse pills?"

"You have an infection in your bladder which would add to your misery if we didn't give you antibiotics." He nodded.

I thought of the meeting I'd had with the family two days previously. All, except for the son from Florida who drank too much, agreed on my approach to their father's care.

I told John, "I'm a little worried about your boy from Miami. He buttonholed me in the hall and wanted a guarantee that I was doing all I could to keep you alive. He insisted I send you to a center where more tests and CAT scans could be done. What do you think about that?"

"God almighty, I've told everyone I don't want to be moved. After our talk Ethel knows that I'm happy and ready to go. That boy never gave a shit about me when I was healthy. If he tries to push you around, just tell him to go to hell."

"Can't do that, John. He'd take me to court," I replied.

"Well then, screw him. He's not the one that's dying."

Now there was a real chill in the air around Dead Indian Dome and I stood up, put away my writing pad, and stretched. A week after that last talk, the skin over John's tailbone broke down and became infected. He was comatose and in no pain, but I had to send him to the hospital for IV antibiotics. I hated to do it, but the Florida son was threatening legal action against the nursing home.

The sun had set, but the last rays painted scarlet the flat-bottomed clouds scattered above the silhouette of the mountains. An echelon of Canada geese honked their way to grassy ponds on the Randall place, and twilight's cool wind made me zip up my jacket. I strained to see the outline of the stream as it coursed among the cotton-woods and fancied I could make out a tall figure in hip boots hobbling slowly along the bank. And then, as a shaggy black dog caught up and followed at his heels, a distant voice settled in my ear.

Found a great little creek here. And guess what, your ol' black dog fishes with me all the time. Showed up about a year ago. Said he got a hell of a disease, and you did all you could to save him. The day came when he couldn't fish with you, or even eat anymore. Couldn't hardly walk. Lost control of himself at night and started to wet his corner of your bed. Told me you carried him out and helped him stand by a tree and fed him raw hamburger—his favorite. When you couldn't stand his pain anymore, your young veterinary friend came to the bedroom and gave him a shot while you held his head in your hands. He told me you really lost it then. You'd been crying your heart out when he left to come here.

So cheer up, Doc. He's my great buddy, too. Still makes gas to beat the band, but now it smells like sage after the rain. When it's your time, we'll both be waiting. And I'll leave a few of the big ones for you.

Epilogue

SOMETIMES, on walks with my dogs or when fishing a mountain stream, I think about the places I've been and the people I've met.

I think of Maria, an uncomplicated, serene young Puerto Rican woman, living in the desperate slums of New York's inner city. She taught me the truth that the majesty in human spirit could bloom in squalor. She taught me to look for that, whatever the surroundings.

I thought of the old Belgian surgeon who operated bitterly on a humanity that gave no thanks. His pride kept him duty bound, and his love focused on an Arabian stallion he had to abandon. He taught me that duty by itself, without love, yields loneliness and a sour soul.

I learned from a kid who fell from a mango tree and the boy with the broken leg that the thrill of accomplishment can sometimes dull performance if pride hurries routine or clouds judgment.

Chuck showed me the value of listening, and John the importance of an *acte de présence*.

Today, our medical schools are filled with young men and women who want to be part of a profession that combines scientific excellence with a deep understanding of human nature and its needs and challenges. They are the ones who keep my adrenals fired up. They give me reasons to be optimistic about the future of our profession.

Patients will always want and need technically competent physicians and surgeons who make the time to listen and understand. Patients will be our profession's strongest allies if they see us as advocates in their care rather than instruments manipulated by the business of medicine.

My old Swiss friend and mentor, Professor Vannotti, told me, "Adventure is never planned. It is marching through the door of opportunity into the unknown, with enthusiasm. You endured the storms and built up something extraordinaire in an impossible place. Now you must go to your mountains in Wyoming; look back, and look forward, and write. Write so people feel what you have felt, and so people will see what you have seen. And be with your family."

I hope this book opens the hearts and broadens the perspectives of those who read it, for then my old friend's expectations will have been met.

Acknowledgments

First and foremost is my gratitude to the innumerable friends, patients and colleagues who have helped to make my life as a doctor the fulfillment of dreams seeded in reality.

My life-long gratitude to Tine, my wife of fifty-eight years. Her partnership and love have been like the hidden pillars that support a home or a hospital.

Many thanks to my daughter, Glenn, for her gracious foreword.

Thanks to Deanne Bradley, RN. Our practice has been known as "Dea and Doc" for over twenty years.

Much gratitude to Susan Lehr, an assistant extraordinaire, with whom I have worked for fourteen years in the practice and in the production of other books and many other projects.

Happy thanks to our publishing and production team:

Gail Kearns and Penny Paine, production coordinators/publishing consultants. That is their official title. Gail is also an editor who pushes all the best buttons; "Practical Penny," has the skill to give legs to ideas.

Thanks to Peri Poloni who designed the cover. The picture of me looking back was taken by Carole Bardin in her Pinedale, Wyoming studio.

My gratitude also to Christine Nolt, our book designer, and Itoko Maeno who brought our Meadowlark Springs logo to life.

To work with high quality, pleasant professionals is one of the great pluses of independent publishing.

Quick Order Form

Fax orders: (307) 276-5276. Fax this form.

Telephone orders: Call 877-505-0774 (toll free)

email orders: wtclose@trib.com

Postal Orders: Meadowlark Springs Productions, P.O. Box 4460, Marbleton, Wyoming 83113

I would like to order _____ copies of *A Doctor's Life: Unique Stories* @ $15.95 each. (For quantity discounts and special sales please call our toll-free number.)

Name: _____

Address: _____

City: _____ State: _____ Zip: _____

Telephone: _____

email address: _____

Sales tax: Please add 4% for books shipped to Wyoming addresses.

Shipping by air: US: $4.00 for the first book and $2.00 for each additional book.

International: $9.00 for the first book and $5.00 for each additional book (estimate).

Payment: ☐ Check

           ☐ Visa   ☐ MasterCard

Card number: _____ Exp. date: _____

Name on card: _____

THANK YOU FOR YOUR ORDER!